Isle of the Displaced

AN ITALIAN-SCOT'S MEMOIRS OF INTERNMENT DURING THE SECOND WORLD WAR

JOE PIERI

NEIL WILSON PUBLISHING

Published by Neil Wilson Publishing Ltd
303a The Pentagon Centre
36 Washington Street
GLASGOW
G3 8AZ
Tel: 0141-221-1117
Fax: 0141-221-5363
E-mail: nwp@cqm.co.uk
http://www.nwp.co.uk/

© Joe Pieri, 1997

The author has established his moral right to be identified as the author of this work.
A catalogue record for this book is available from the British Library.

ISBN 1-897784-57-0

Typeset in 9/13pt Lucida Bright by Janet Watson, Glasgow

Printed by WSOY, Finland

Acknowledgements
I am indebted to George Martinez of Romsey for encouraging me to write this book. His recollections of some of the events recounted here have been of great help. I thank him also for the ground maps of the camp.

The events in this book took place precisely as I remember them. In some instances I have seen fit to change the names of some persons.

The group photograph on the front jacket shows me seated second from the left, front row. On my right is Giulio Ghiloni from Glasgow and to my left, Mario Casci from Largs. Standing in the back row on the left is Joe Guidi of Glasgow (now dead) who helped me in the tunnel incident (see chapter 20) and to his left, Peter Landi from Bournemouth. Fourth from the left is Joe Salotti, from Prestwick.

Contents

	Introduction	v
1	Origins	1
2	Allegiances	7
3	Arrest	12
4	Woodhouselea	20
5	Warth Mills	25
6	The Ettrick	29
7	Division	34
8	Reception	40
9	Ile Sainte Hélène	48
10	Mutiny	55
11	Negotiation	61
12	Tension	66
13	Mr Paterson	72
14	Work	80
15	Recreation	85
16	Health	94
17	Language	100
18	Escape	108
19	O'Connor	120
20	Finale	128
21	Return	135
22	Aftermath	140
23	Endings	145
	Epilogue	150

To Mary Cameron

Introduction

In the year 1535 the French explorer Jacques Cartier sailed up the St. Lawrence River, landed at a Huron Indian village known as Hochelaga by the natives and gave it the name Mont Real. In 1611 Champlain, the first Governor of French Canada, set up a military post on an island in the middle of the river directly in front of Mont Real which was by now a settlement of some considerable size. He named the island Ile Saint Hélène, after his young bride of that name. Shortly afterwards a fortress was built there and to this day the stark pile of stone and rock still stands. The building is a low edifice of two stories, built of massive stone blocks and encompasses on three sides a narrow courtyard facing out to the river. On the far side lies the main area of Montreal city rising to the imposing heights of Mount Royal beyond.

The island is now a beautifully kept public park much frequented for picnics in the summer by the citizens of Montreal and by tourists who come to enjoy the handsome gardens and the spectacular views of the modern city across the river. The fort serves as a museum. The interior is a series of rather uninteresting military exhibits with pictorial displays portraying the military history of the province of Quebec. These are labelled in English and French. At the end of one of the long and narrow second floor rooms, incongruously set amongst the military exhibits, are three wooden prison cells with iron barred doors. They are small and cramped, measuring some nine by five feet and affixed to one of them is a plaque with an inscription.

> *During the Second World War this fortress served as a prisoner of war camp for Nazi and Fascist prisoners. These are the punishment cells used for the more dangerous of them.*

I spent three years in that camp and 30 days in those cells. This is the story of how I came to be there.

1
Origins

A few kilometres from the hilltop town of Barga in Tuscany, on the steep wooded slopes above, stand the ruins of a small stone chapel. In front is a paved clearing, and on either side a farmhouse and some small barns. The area is remote, deserted and access is difficult. There is no road, but the climb up from Barga is well worth the effort, for the view from the clearing down into the valley beneath is spectacular. Since the end of the 1939-45 war I have trekked up there many times, although the walk seems to become ever steeper for me as the years go by.

Many years ago a family of crofters eked out a living there. The hamlet went by the name of Bacchionero ('Black Wood'), and this is where I was born nearly 80 years ago, at the end of the 1914-18 war.

In the second half of the 19th century, newly developing means of transportation by land and sea had helped to give rise to the social and historical phenomenon of mass emigration from Europe to the sparsely populated lands of the Americas. Every European country contributed to the flow of immigrants seeking a better life in the New World, none more so than the emergent nation of Italy.

With hunger, poverty and social injustice at home as the spur, a massive flow of millions of Italians began to make its way to far-off lands offering wealth and opportunity. Until the unification of Italy in 1861 no statistics were available to catalogue such an unprecedented movement of people, but between 1880 and 1890 it is recorded that some five million Italians left their homeland to seek a better life. In the first 20 years of the 20th century a staggering total of ten million souls quit their native Italian regions to settle for the main part in the USA and the countries of South America.

ISLE OF THE DISPLACED

My family was one such.

My parents, Francesco and Maria Pieri were a young couple from the Barga area near Lucca. To escape the grinding poverty of their native hills they set off in the early 1900s for the USA and after the shock and bewilderment aroused by the sight of Ellis Island and the teeming tenements of New York, they found that life was good, for if a man had a strong and willing back there was plenty of well-paid work available. A series of jobs in different places followed, with the young couple finally settling in St Paul, Minnesota, where my older brother Ralph was born.

Around 1912, at the time of her North African campaigns and with her manpower depleted by the mass exodus of her young men in previous years, Italy mounted a wide-ranging recruitment campaign among Italians of military age in the USA. Beguiled by glowing promises of a better future, my parents decided to return to Italy and my father served in the campaign in Libya until the outbreak of the 1914-18 war. Then, in 1915, Italy joined Britain and France and declared war on Germany.

My father was lucky to escape the carnage of the battlefields of Caporetto and the Piave. Caporetto had been a particularly bloody but lucky experience for him. Subjected to days of ceaseless and heavy artillery attack, without food and water and outflanked by the rapidly advancing Austrians, the Italian troops began a disorderly retreat down the mountain passes. The officer in command, General Cadorna, stopped the retreat from becoming a disastrous rout by issuing orders that, *pour encourager les autres*, every tenth man found retreating and without arms would be summarily shot. Francesco was lucky in that he did his numbers and had held on to his rifle. It is interesting to note that a senior officer in the Austrian forces who had tried out this new kind of Blitzkrieg was a certain Major Erwin Rommel, who was to achieve fame in the North African desert 25 years later. For his part in the Caporetto attack Rommel was awarded the *Pour Le Mérite* (the 'Blue Max'), the highest decoration in the German army of the 1914-18 war.

Francesco returned to his native Tuscany after the armistice in 1918, but disillusionment soon set in. The old ways had not changed, the ossified social structure still held sway, and the abysmal poverty from which Francesco had sought to escape still existed. Nothing had changed, indeed, conditions were worse.

There was little work to be had, and the chaotic politics of the day, with bitter quarrels raging between the differing groups of Monarchists, Bolsheviks and the newly-emerged *Fascisti* led by one Benito Mussolini, held out no hope of material progress. So once more Francesco's thoughts turned to the USA, but the way there was now barred. Immediately after the war in 1919, faced with the prospect of a new and unmanageable influx of immigrants from Europe, the United States government had imposed a quota system of immigration which severely limited the entry of Mediterranean peoples. No matter that Francesco had lived and worked in there for a number of years before the war or that Ralph was American by birth; he would have to take his place in the queue, which meant a wait of many, many years.

By this time I had arrived on the scene, and my father was faced with the bleak prospect of scratching a living in Bacchionero to feed himself and his family. So with the door to America closed, he set about searching for another place where hard work and effort would be rewarded. But where to go? And how to get there? Francesco turned to the one agency which could offer help — the Church. The local priest, who came to say Mass in the little chapel every Sunday for the benefit of the many crofters who lived in the neighbouring hills, was consulted. He was well-informed in these matters, and spoke of a city called Glasgow in the country of Scotland in the far north of Britain. A number of families from the district had found jobs there, and it was reported to be a good place to live. Work was still to be had there, and there were as yet no travel restrictions to that part of the world. So the decision was made, and with the promise of work and lodgings from an Italian family already established there, my father and mother packed their few belongings, wrapped us up to face the reported rigours of the Scottish weather and set off on the four-day journey to Glasgow.

By comparison to the massive flow of emigration to the Americas, the number of Italians who came to settle in Britain was minute, and their distribution in the country followed no set pattern. The majority, of course, settled in the London area, where the cosmopolitan atmosphere acted as a magnet, but scattered throughout the land there was hardly a city, town or village which did not boast of an Italian café or fish and chip shop. In Scotland, in the industrial belt between Glasgow and Edinburgh, hundreds of Italian families made their home and became a familiar part of the Scottish scene. It is difficult now, given the range of social services available in a modern society, to appreciate the hardship and privation faced by those immigrant families with no welfare state, no social security and no one to turn to if health failed or strength waned. In a strange land you depended on your own family in times of need.

My father however was relatively lucky. His years in America had left him with a fair amount of English, although heavily accented, and in no time he was able to cope adequately with the accents of the Glasgwegians. Moreover, placenames like Kilmarnock, Aberfoyle and Auchinleck were already familiar to him, for at the time of the collapse of the Italian army on the Caporetto front, some Scottish regiments had been sent to stiffen Italian resistance there, and he had fought side by side with men from such places.

So the Pieri family started a new life in Glasgow. My father's work was that of a fish fryer in a family-owned restaurant on the edge of the city centre, and although the working day was 12 hours long, and the week was six days long, it was not as heavy and as concentrated as some of the work he had known in America. By the standards of the day his weekly wage of £3 was adequate and each week a few shillings would be set aside towards the day when he would be able to set up a little shop of his own, for that was the dream of every Italian immigrant: a business of your own, a home of your own.

For myself and my brother a strangely dichotomous way of life had begun. We were language perfect in Glasgow English, so we merged well into the Scottish environment. But then after school hours our surroundings at home were of a purely Italian nature, where only Italian was spoken, so my brother and I grew up completely bilingual. We could slip easily and effortlessly from one language to the other and from one set of cultural values to the other, but we were at all times aware of the difference in origin between ourselves, our school companions and our Scottish neighbours.

To some extent this feeling of displacement, I suppose, could well have been created by us. The language barrier and the wide cultural differences between Tuscan and Glasgwegian made close contact with the locals difficult for our parents. For them socialising was limited to the occasional Sunday visit to one or other of the few Italian families in the neighbourhood, and my brother and I were never actively encouraged to introduce outsiders into the family circle. By the same token, I cannot remember ever having been invited into a local household as a boy.

However, I played quite happily with the other children in the street; at that age there are no racial or religious inhibitions. These come later in life, and have much to do with bias acquired from the society in which we live. We lived in a rented house on the fringes of the Gorbals, the Glasgow slum and went to school at St Francis, a Catholic school in the area. In the playground many a taunt of 'dirty wee Tally' had to be answered in scuffles and fist fights, yet after school hours we would have to stand shoulder to shoulder with our tormentors from school in common cause against gangs of children from other schools in the same area. Those were the days when religion was much more polarised than it is now and you had to be ready with some sort of answer when challenged by the cry, 'Are you a Billy or a Dan or an old Tin Can?'[1] and if the opposing gangs were bigger and stronger, woe betide you if you were not fleeter of foot.

Those were the days of the infamous Glasgow gangs, of which the Gorbals had more than its fair share and youngsters would model themselves on gangs with names like San Toy, The Billy Boys, The Cumbies. My brother and I were sternly ordered not to mix with *i loffari Scozzesi*[2] and to come home straight from school, but it was impossible to avoid all contact with them and many were the cuts and bruises tended to by a tearful mother who said the rosary daily and prayed that the family might find a better place to live.

I now often think about those days and wonder whether it might have been better to have grown up in the poor Tuscan hills rather than on the edge of a Gorbals slum. My conclusion is always that it is easier to rise and prosper from a slum than to have lived in a society which offered no opportunity and would almost certainly have claimed my brother and myself as cannon fodder for a Fascist army.

In retrospect, I suppose that in a sense we were the Pakistani immigrants of our day, tolerated but not quite accepted by our neighbours. We were aliens who gave services to the community in the form of cafés and fish and chip shops which the locals themselves did not provide, and we progressed by dint of long and hard

---

[1] 'Are you a Protestant, a Catholic or a Jew?'
[2] Scottish good-for-nothings.

hours of work. Integration, however, for us was easier; the colour of our skins was the same as that of our neighbours.

Hard work began to show rewards. By the early 1930s, despite the Depression which had created millions of unemployed, the family began to prosper. By this time my father's dream had come true and he was now the proud owner of a little fish and chip shop in a suburb of Glasgow, with the family living in a rented apartment far from the squalor of the Gorbals. With very little education of his own, my father's values did not include the desire for a lengthy education for his sons, so Ralph had left school at the age of 14, to be joined behind the shop counter by myself when I too reached school-leaving age.

By this time I was in third year at St Mungo's Academy in the tough Townhead area. I was fairly good academically and even better at dealing physically with any 'dirty Tally' taunt, and I suppose that had I pressed my parents I could have continued my education there. But to what end? Become a teacher? The idea of having to stand in a classroom all day long endlessly repeating the same lesson did not appeal to me. A doctor? I remembered from my early childhood days the kindly figure of Dr Easterman and his periodic visits to us. After his diagnosis, usually measles or chicken-pox, a ritual glass of vermouth would be offered and partaken of, and his five-shilling fee, discreetly left at the edge of the table, pocketed. In later years I was to see him as a worn-out figure, aged in his service to others, and that vision also did not inspire me. Without a family tradition of education I had no appreciation of the intrinsic value of learning.

But I was becoming aware of the wider world around me and what a half crown in your pocket could do for you materially and for your self-esteem. The foundation for a financially rewarding future had been laid by my father's sweat and effort. I had no objection at all when he suggested that I go to work beside my brother.

2
Allegiances

By the year 1938 the family had attained a modest level of success. My brother and I had become the driving forces in the business, and the first shop was sold and replaced by one of great potential near the city centre. Ralph, my American-born brother, had married and set up house with his wife, Teresa Nicoletti, the daughter of a Glasgow-Italian family. The idea of a liaison with any except an Italian girl was anathema, especially to our mother, who would shake her head in deep disapproval on hearing of any marriage of an Italian to a local. There would be a heavenward rolling of eyeballs and a solemn wringing of hands. Such a union could lead only to disaster, she would intone, and no good could ever come of such a marriage. All of which served only to perpetuate our sense of alienation from the locals.

By this time the years of deprivation and hard work of my father's youth were beginning to have an effect on his health, and he started to talk of retirement. He had one close Scottish friend, Alex McCrea, a sergeant in the Glasgow police; a friendship which had started in 1917 on the Austro-Italian war front. Black Alex, as he was known, was in one of the Scottish regiments sent to Italy in that year, and the two men had fought side by side and shared many a hardship.

My father had spent almost all of his working life outside Italy and had lost all desire to return permanently to the land of his birth. Moreover, he was an old-fashioned socialist in his political views, and these would not have been welcome in a land now in the grip of the Fascists. He had grown to love the way of life in Scotland, so he consulted Alex on the question of his retirement and he was promptly advised to apply for British citizenship. He made the necessary application, with Alex as sponsor, and he became a British citizen in August 1939, just one month before the outbreak of war.

By the age of 20 I had become a voracious reader, and was well aware of my position as a foreigner and as a possible future enemy alien. All the indications seemed to point to war between Germany and Britain, with Italy as an ally of Hitler, and because I was now the only Italian in the family, at times I too considered an application for British citizenship. Why did I not follow in my father's footsteps and swear allegiance to the British flag? After all, acceptance was certain: I had lived in Britain for 18 of my 21 years, had no political leanings and no blemish on my character, but I elected to remain as I was born. After the passage of almost 60 years it is probably impossible to analyse with any degree of accuracy the personal motives for decisions made so long ago, but as far as I can remember, and I believe my memory to be sound, my reasoning went as follows.

Despite my almost purely Scottish lifestyle, I just did not feel British. Almost daily I was reminded of the fact that I was an Italian. The 1930s had been a period of political turmoil in Europe. Italy's invasion of Abyssinia and Mussolini's intervention in the Spanish Civil War had created a wave of ill feeling against Italy in the general population. The childhood taunts of 'dirty wee Tally' had given way to more frequent, forceful and insulting remarks about my nationality from some of the more drunken and belligerent types who made up a good percentage of our night-time clientele. 'Dirty wee Tally' had given way to 'Tally bastard'. Not that these people knew me or anything about my background, I could just as easily have been Scottish, or French or any one of a dozen different nationalities. But I had a chip shop. Only Italians had chip shops, ergo I must have been an Italian. These remarks bothered me no more than the weather did, they were part and parcel of my environment.

I encountered more discreet and polite discrimination at the other end of the social spectrum. A foreign name could guarantee blackballing from a club membership and even the better educated of my acquaintances, with absolutely no malice intended, could make the odd remark which would place me firmly in an Italian context.

'Are you going home for your holidays, Joe?'

'Do you think you'll go back to live in Italy, Joe?'
'You should do something about Mussolini, Joe.'
Our shop consumed a fair quantity of raw materials, and our custom would be much sought after by the various suppliers.
'Must have you and Ralph out for a meal sometime, Joe.'
'Must have you out for a round of golf at the club, Joe.'
'Must have you out to the house sometime, Joe.'

Empty phrases, and all for the sake of doing some business. The golf clubs mentioned had never been trodden by Jewish, Italian, or for that matter Catholic feet. This type of xenophobia pricked the skin a little, where the 'Tally bastard' variety did not.

We are what we are because of two factors: genetic inheritance and environmental influence, and the latter in my formative years were hardly calculated to make me feel British in spirit. But Glasgow was my home, the place where I earned a living and the place where my family lived. I realised this, but failed to see how a signature on a piece of paper swearing allegiance to a King and to a flag could make me any different or better than I was.

I could see no point in becoming a full member of a society to which spiritually I could not fully belong. But neither did I owe any allegiance whatsoever to the land of my birth. As a teenager I had been to Italy on a few occasions to visit my grandparents and other relatives, and had lived there once for a full year. I felt vague stirrings of embarrassment and dislike for the bombast and loud rhetoric of Mussolini. I could see clearly that the way of life and social structure in Britain was far superior to the class-ridden and still impoverished Italy of those days. But even in the land of my birth I was not accepted as one of themselves. In Glasgow I was 'The Tally'. In Barga I was *'Lo Scozzese'*, the Scotsman. The lines from *The Lay of the Last Minstrel* by Sir Walter Scott could well have been written for the likes of me.

> *Breathes there the man, with soul so dead,*
> *Who never to himself hath said,*
> *This is my own, my native land!*

If I did become a British subject would the slights and the insults cease? Would my way of life change in any way? Would I have been any more acceptable socially? I thought not. Moreover, the fact that as a British subject I would have had to do military service was probably the most important factor in my decision to remain as I was. I had no wish to be conscripted into the British Army. It was clear that if war did come Italy would be on the side of Germany against Britain, and I had no desire to be placed in the position of possibly having to fight against cousins and relations already serving in the Italian Army. The sight of my many Scottish friends now in uniform troubled me somewhat, but they did not seem to mind that I remained a civilian. As a matter of fact some voiced the opinion that as an Italian I was lucky to be exempt from conscription. I went over all this with my father and brother, who, from a business point of view, obviously did not want me to do military service. And so I agonised, vacillated, rationalised and remained as I was.

But then came Germany's invasion of Poland and Britain's eventual declaration of war, so I began to worry about what would happen if Italy were to join in. Weeks went by and I reasoned that the danger had passed. If Mussolini had wanted war he would have joined in from the beginning, I argued. Besides, nothing would happen to me in any event; I had no political connections, and I had no dealings with the *Casa del Fascio*, the Fascist social club in Park Circus organised by the Italian Consul for the benefit of Italians in Scotland. Some of my older Scottish acquaintances spoke of the internment of Germans during the 1914-18 war, but I discounted that possibility as being just inconceivable in my case. So I applied myself single-mindedly to the business, bothered no one, and kept my head firmly buried in the sand.

In the few months after the beginning of the war life changed dramatically for the people of Glasgow. There was an air of tension all around. A complete blackout had been imposed during the hours of darkness, and no chink of light was allowed to escape from the heavily-curtained shops and houses. Cars were fitted with headlamp covers to emit only a thin sliver of light, tramcars in complete darkness inched their way along the pitch-black streets and during the long, dark and often fog-bound winter nights the city ground to a standstill.

Gas masks had been issued to everyone, air raid shelters were signposted, and parks and private gardens were equipped with Anderson shelters (so named after Sir John Anderson, the Home Secretary at that time). These were arched, corrugated-iron structures dug into the ground and protected by sandbags, to serve as civilian shelters in the event of air raids. To protect against incendiary raids, huge static water tanks had been installed in every street.

Military convoys rumbled occasionally through the city. Fat balloon barrages wallowed over tenement roofs, presumably to protect against low-flying aircraft. Strange uniforms and sounds appeared in the Glasgow streets: English soldiers with unaccustomed accents, French sailors with red pom-pom blue berets; French mountain regiments, the Chasseurs Alpins with their floppy black berets; Algerian Goums with baggy white trousers, fierce dark faces and red hats. All these and more thronged the Glasgow streets, pubs and restaurants. The city throbbed with an excitement and glamour never before experienced.

War is always good for trade. Money flowed freely, the slump and misery of the 1930s had vanished and life seemed somehow to be sharper, more purposeful and exciting. The war fronts on the continent seemed unreal and far away, with Germany and the Allies safely ensconced behind their respective Siegfried and Maginot lines.

We're gonna hang out our washing on the Siegfried Line, went the popular song of the day, with the lyrics reflecting the almost frivolous mood of the general public. I too was caught up in this atmosphere. Business boomed, the family restaurant was filled to capacity daily, and money flowed into the till as never before. I no longer worried about my position as an Italian. The German invasion of Poland would soon be forgotten, the affair would fizzle out with some kind of international agreement and life would go on as before.

3
Arrest

Suddenly, at the beginning of May 1940, all the euphoria vanished. Germany invaded Denmark and Norway and the so-called 'phoney war' became only too real. The impregnable Maginot Line crumbled under the sudden impact of Blitzkrieg: the German Panzer tank divisions had a speed and power never seen before in war and the Allied armies disintegrated under the combined attacks of tanks and Stuka bombers. After ten days of this devastating warfare the French army had been destroyed and Lord Gort, leader of the British expeditionary forces, began to plan the evacuation of the remnants of his army from Dunkirk.

By June 4 the evacuation from France had been successfully completed, the Germans were in control of most of France, and on June 10, Hitler's ally Benito Mussolini, in haste to be in at the kill, declared war on Britain and France. At that point some 19,000 Italian residents in Britain became enemy aliens. These people posed a considerable problem to the British Government. Although the majority were of no conceivable danger to the British war effort, a good percentage were of military age and could possibly have constituted a dangerous 'fifth column' in the event of an Axis invasion of Britain. The words had a pertinent and sinister meaning having originated in the Spanish Civil War. When Franco began his advance on Madrid in July 1936 with four columns of rebel soldiers, the garrison of the Alcazar in Toledo came under siege by government troops. Franco was advised by his generals not to divert to Toledo to relieve the rebels, since the delay would enable Madrid to organise its defences. This advice was rejected by him with the remark that he had a fifth column of hidden rebels in the capital which would rise at the appropriate time and help subdue the city.

ARREST

Non-existent though this column proved to be, the words were taken up and frequently used in Britain to assume the existence of Fascist and Nazi sympathisers who would rise and give support to invading forces.

Moreover, Britain faced the problem of a huge influx of refugees at the time of the fall of France and the Low Countries. Thousands of refugees, both Jews and Gentiles, had fled to England in the frantic days before Dunkirk, and who was to deny the possibility that in this mass of human jetsam there may have been many deliberately planted to carry out acts of sabotage during an invasion of Britain? On the day of Italy's declaration of war, the question of the internment of Italians came up during a meeting of the British War Cabinet, and the problem of separating the obviously harmless from the potentially dangerous was discussed. At the end of the meeting Churchill is reported to have issued the following short sharp order: 'Collar the lot!' An order went out to all police stations in Great Britain that all male Italians between the age of 16 and 70 should be arrested immediately and interned.

June 10 dawned warm and sunny. I went about my affairs listlessly. For many days business had been bad, all the soldiers had vanished from the streets and after business hours people rushed home to their wireless sets to keep abreast of the constantly unfolding news from the war fronts. The BBC announcer's voice broke through my reveries '. . .and so a state of war now exists between Britain and Italy'.

I stood blankly trying to digest this information. A tall figure in policeman's uniform appeared at the door.

'Hello Joe, you'll have heard the news?' It was Alex McCrae, my father's old friend. 'I shouldn't be telling you this, and I'm sorry about it, but you're up for arrest during the night', he continued. I looked at him in amazement.

'What for?'

'For internment, that's what for. There's a big list of you people up in the police Station. I think you'd better close up, you never know what's going to happen.'

The bottom seemed to have dropped out of my world. All my self-deception and confidence had evaporated at Alex's words.

'Don't you be telling anyone now. . . we're not supposed to let anyone know. Don't worry, you'll be all right', he assured me.

And with a slap on my back, the big policeman left, but a cold and heavy hand seemed to have settled on my stomach. I quickly shut up shop and proceeded to dismiss the staff, telling them to come back next morning; I was quite touched at the emotional and tearful reaction of some of the waitresses. I climbed slowly and pensively up the tenement steps to our home directly above the shop, not wanting to believe the events of the last few moments, then sat wondering what to do next. My parents were on holiday in Rothesay, a seaside resort on the isle of Bute in the Clyde estuary, but very few houses had phones in those days, so there was no way I could get in touch with them. I'll go and see Ralph now, I thought, and discuss matters with him, but first I decided to pack some belongings in a suitcase in readiness for the arrest I had been told was imminent.

A muted roar made itself heard from the street below, rising to a crescendo of shouting voices directly under my window. I went over and peered out. A crowd of about a hundred shouting and gesticulating people, pushing in front of them a handcart loaded with stones and bricks, were gathering in front of the shop. 'There's a Tally place... do it in!', came the shout; then to an accompaniment of yells and cheers, a barrage of missiles came flying through the air, smashing into the glass frontage of the shop. A dozen or so of the mob, armed with sticks and batons, cleared away the jagged edges of the broken windows and jumped through into the shop beyond. Through a curiously detached and dreamlike mental haze I could hear the sound of smashing and curses from below and peering fearfully through the lace curtains, I watched as the contents of the looted shop were distributed to the milling crowd. That night there were few, if any, Italian shops left untouched by the gangs of hooligans, and although no physical harm was done to anyone, years of hard work was destroyed by unrestrained bands of louts who roamed the streets of Glasgow wrecking and looting in the name of patriotism. As far as I know, not a finger was lifted by the police in an attempt to stop the looting of Italian shops in Glasgow that night.

However, one Italian shop was neither smashed nor looted. In Maitland Street in the heart of the Cowcaddens district, Big Emma ran a small fish and chip shop. A massive 6ft in height and as strong as an ox, Emma, who hailed from the Lucca district in Tuscany, had

ARREST

recently been widowed, but continued to run her little shop in order to maintain herself and infant son. Her massive presence brooked no nonsense from her rough and often drunken customers, and Big Emma and her wee shop had become something of an institution in the area. As a crowd of drunken hooligans, bent on destruction, swirled round her shop, she snatched up a heavy metal chip basket in a meaty hand and rushed out to confront the noisy crowd at her door.

'You bastards', she roared in a thickly-accented Glasgow-Italian cry, 'Don't you touch anything. You would eat shite if I fried it!'

This magnificent *non sequitur* stopped the crowd dead in its tracks. A hush descended, then a laugh rippled through the crowd and a voice rang out,

'Come on away. You'se canny touch hur, she's a wumman'. The crowd simmered slowly for a while and then moved on. Big Emma and her shop were left in peace for the duration of the war and did a roaring trade selling items of a more traditional nature to her hungry customers.

The evening dragged on into night. I had been afraid to venture out after witnessing the looting of our shop and had abandoned any idea of going to see my brother. I was dozing fitfully on a chair until jerked alert by the sound of a sharp knock at the door. I opened it cautiously and somewhat fearfully. Two uniformed policemen stood there.

'Are you Joe Pieri?'

I could not deny it.

'Get some things together and come with us'.

On the night of June 10 there was hardly a family of Italian origin in Britain, irrespective of social status or political leanings, which did not suffer the summary arrest of their men in the age bracket intended and indeed in some cases outside it, as will be seen later. The draconian roundup of civilians without charge and without the slightest attempt at justification left scars on the great majority of Italian families throughout Britain and led to tragedy from which some never recovered.

Under the system of police registration of aliens introduced in 1920, every alien in each district was registered and known to the local police. A certificate of registration with photograph and relevant particulars had to be produced on demand, and onto this certificate every movement of the alien, change of address, change of employment, had to be entered. Under this system there should have been no difficulty in identifying potentially dangerous individuals. There were not that many families with Italian names in Scotland, a few hundred at most, and many of these were second and third generation immigrants. Nine months of war had already been waged with Germany before Mussolini saw fit to enter, surely enough for a thorough check to be made on any prospective internee? A selective internment of dangerous elements, yes, but the indiscriminate round up of Italians on June 10, 1940 is difficult to understand. Unjust and unfair in retrospect perhaps, but then of course, the mortal danger which faced Britain in 1940 was presumably justification enough for the swiftness and expediency of the action.

The Northern police station was to be found in the run-down heart of the Cowcaddens, a dark grey stone building with well-worn steps leading up to a heavy wooden door through which passed daily a steady stream of humanity fallen foul of the law. Pimps and prostitutes, housebreakers, wife beaters, thieves and violent drunks were its usual visitors, but on the day after Italy's declaration of war a new kind of prisoner occupied the well-used basement cells. About 35 Italians of all ages sat miserably in the cramped rooms. The arrests had been swift and efficient, and apart from myself probably no one had expected a knock at the door during the small hours of the night which startled into wakefulness confused and apprehensive men and women, the men to be taken away and the women to be left weeping. Waiting outside each door would be a Black Maria, dull black-painted vans used for the transportation of prisoners, which disgorged their cargo of Italians at various police stations throughout the city.

The cells of the police station in Maitland Street were typical of the sort of accommodation given to prisoners. Small rooms of about ten foot by ten, they had iron doors with small inspection hatches in the centre, walls of white glazed brick and floors of polished stone slats. At each side of the cell were two raised concrete shelves on which were placed thin mattresses issued at the time of arrest, to serve as beds during the night. There was a lavatory pan and since this could be flushed only from the outside passage, excreta would often lie for hours until attended to by a passing guard.

ARREST

There was no heating, and even with the warm weather outside, the walls were cold and dank. An all-pervading stink of stale sweat and urine hung permanently in the air and seemed to have permeated the very fabric of the cells. Into one of these rooms, I and three others were ushered unceremoniously. One of my cellmates was particularly agitated. Aldo Girasole, a young Glaswegian-Italian in his late twenties, was to be married the next day, but was instead stuck in a prison cell with no inkling of what the future might hold and with no means of informing his bride to be of his predicament.

For three days the four of us were kept there without contact with the outside world. No information of any kind was given and the guards who brought plain but ample food twice a day gave only monosyllabic and non-committal answers to the flow of questions put to them. Why don't you let us know something? Why doesn't someone tell us what's going to happen? The bloody criminals at least know what they're supposed to have done! Don't we have the same rights as they have? Our relatives were kept as much in the dark as we were. The police stations were besieged by frantic relatives seeking news of their loved ones, but no information was given as to the whereabouts of the arrested men. The only comment was to the effect that the men were being well cared for and that soon the relatives would be informed as to future events. In vain lawyers were hurriedly consulted: this was war time, and the normal process of the law no longer applied. With that the anxious families had to be content.

On the morning of the fourth day the cell door was thrown open and the weary four of us, frustrated and angry after our days of confinement, were brusquely ordered out. Our belongings were returned to us, and then we were escorted on to a waiting Black Maria. Once in motion, our route took us past the Savoy, our family shop, and through the barred windows of the police van I could see that the smashed frontage had been boarded up. Strangely enough the sight of the wreckage of years of hard family work aroused no emotion in me whatsoever.

For four days Maryhill Barracks was put to use as a makeshift internment camp. From all of the police stations in the Glasgow area, Black Marias shuttled back and forth with cargoes of prisoners to be handed over to the military authorities. Blankets and palliasses were issued, sergeants and soldiers barked orders and the docile mass of prisoners formed into groups, friends staying close to friends and relations to relations.

A more motley crew would have been hard to imagine. The ages seemed to range from the very young to bent old men, with the only common denominator being the possession of an Italian name. All social groups seemed to be represented, with some dressed in rough working clothes and others well-clad in expensive tailored suits. Some were second generation Italians who could speak only English; some complained loudly about their arrest; some shouted to the soldiers that they had served in the British army during the 1914-18 War; some proclaimed to anyone who would listen that they had relatives now serving in the army, and one elderly weeping, greybeard — Antonio Santangeli — declared to all and sundry that his son was a sergeant serving with the British forces in France.

For all of them, however, the three days they were to spend at the barracks were a welcome change from the atmosphere of the police cells. The air was clean, the food plain but adequate and a limited amount of exercise was possible. Speculation ran riot as to our possible destination. Some of the older men with memories of the 1914-18 war spoke of the Isle of Man where the German civilians had been interned, but it all was guesswork and our questions to the soldiers went unanswered.

On the morning of the fourth day at the barracks, after the usual breakfast of strong tea, bread, margarine and jam, we were told to get all our belongings together, and after a short wait in the compound, we marched out under heavy guard into the street.

Word of the imminent appearance of the prisoners had spread and the pavements were lined with hundreds of curiosity seekers straining to get a view of the marching men. I tried to keep in some sort of step with my companions and keep my head held high. I'm not going to show any fear or despondency to these people, I thought, with the events of that first night still vivid in my mind. But the crowds lining the streets were strangely muted, in sharp contrast to the mobs which had taken to the streets on the night of the arrests, and although a few jeers were shouted at the prisoners, very few voices could be heard above the sound of scuffling feet.

The untidy marching men must have presented a curious sight to the onlookers. Ranging from 16-year-old youths to bent gentlemen in their seventies, wearing clothes which had been slept in for more than a week, we did not seem to constitute much of a threat to anyone. The smartly uniformed soldiers who marched in unison on the outside of the column were in sharp contrast to the listlessly shuffling prisoners. Our destination was a railway siding some 500 yards from the barracks gates in Garrioch Road, and with the short walk soon completed, we were made to assemble on the station platform to await the next leg of our journey.

The day was hot and sunny as we sat and waited, and it seemed to engender a mood of euphoria in us. We chattered and joked and the guards relaxed with us, offering cigarettes and chocolates. On the station platform was a ticket office manned by a solitary, elderly railway employee who stood watching the proceedings. He paused for a while, then came out to the platform, offering a few cigarettes to the waiting prisoners with the words,

'Good luck to you wherever you're going. We're all Jock Tamson's bairns'.

I cannot say whether the thanks directed to him was for the cigarettes or the words of comfort, but the prisoners were profuse in their acknowledgement.

4
Woodhouselea

The train from Glasgow unloaded its cargo of prisoners at Milton Bridge, a small village a few miles south of Edinburgh. We were surrounded by armed guards with bayonets at the ready, and in answer to shouted commands began to march raggedly out of the station and along a narrow country lane. It was hot. Some of the older men became visibly distressed and had to be helped along by their younger companions. So we slowed the pace as much as possible, and ignored the commands and none too gentle shoves of the soldiers. After about an hour's march we came to a perspiring and tired halt. In a district known as Woodhouselea, a makeshift tented camp had been pitched in a grassy field which had been sectioned off with barbed-wire fencing about seven feet high, enclosing scores of tents erected in neat orderly rows. Hundreds of men lay sunning themselves in the spaces between tents and lazily stood up to observe our arrival.

The barbed-wire gates of the camp were dragged open and we walked in one at a time, giving our name to an officer as we passed through. We were then escorted in groups of six to a tent, given blankets and groundsheets and left to our own resources. The slabs of bread and cheese issued on departure from the barracks that morning had long since been eaten, and we tried to bed down for the night with the pangs of hunger added to our general discomfort. An incident then took place which manifested the unselfishness and generosity which was often to show itself among the prisoners in the years to come. With us in the tent was a chap by the name of Dino Orsi, a stoutly built man of about 30 who came from the Maryhill district of Glasgow where he ran a small fish and chip shop. Without a word being said he pulled from his pocket four bars of

Kit Kat chocolate biscuits which he proceeded to share out amongst us. This was a generous gesture, for he could well have consumed the biscuits himself without anyone being the wiser.

The next morning dawned brilliantly, and we were awakened by the clear notes of a loudly blown bugle. The wire gate to the camp had been thrown open to give access to a long row of tables set down immediately outside the wire. On these tables were piled stack upon stack of slabs of bread liberally coated with margarine, and large urns of steaming hot tea. Under heavily-armed guard we filed out for our share of food which we took back behind the wire to eat whilst seated outside our respective tents. With my hunger satisfied I began an exploration of the camp. At the top end of the field latrines had been dug, well removed from the tented area, and these were already doing a brisk business. They were totally inadequate to cope with the long queue of men waiting to use them, so some were simply squatting down near the barbed-wire fence instead.

I then turned my attention to the men already in the camp on our arrival. They were Italian, spoke no English, and did not conform to the Glasgow-Italian types of my experience. I had difficulty in understanding most of them. Their dialects and accents were those of Sardinia, Calabria and Sicily, and it was not until I approached and spoke to one of their officers, a Captain Bonorino, who came from Genoa and who spoke an understandable Italian, that their presence there was explained.

These were the crews of five Italian tramp steamers seized while at anchor in Scottish waters and taken to Woodhouselea, the nearest available detention point. This explained the overcrowding at the camp and the lack of adequate rations. What had been originally intended as a camp for a few hundred civilians was now accommodating about 200 unexpected guests.

I was naive enough to think that in a time of common adversity and misfortune such as faced us at Woodhouselea, men would show a desire to help one another. Any such illusion that I may have had, strengthened as it had been by Dino Orsi's generous sharing of his chocolate bars, was soon to be rudely shattered.

One of the tents near the entrance to the camp housed a certain Mr Renati, a heavily built and flamboyant admirer of *Il Duce*, who owned a café in the south side of Glasgow. His internment could have come as no surprise to him, for he was an avowed Fascist well known in Italian circles for his activities in connection with Il Fascio, the Fascist social club in Park Circus. At the time of the invasion of Abyssinia and the imposition of sanctions on Italy, he had gone the rounds of Italian families in Glasgow asking for gifts of gold to be donated to the consul for shipment back to Italy. The gold was to be used to help offset the economic effects of the sanctions, but the request was not favourably received by some families whose sympathies did not lie entirely with *Il Duce* and his policies.

Renati was the self-appointed morale builder of the camp, and exhorted his fellow prisoners to be of good cheer. All this would not last long, went his message. There was no way, he argued, that Britain could face up to the combined might of Germany and Italy. France had fallen and from now on it would be an easy passage. Britain would soon see the futility of carrying on a hopeless war, he continued, and an armistice of some sort would come about with barely a shot fired. Everyone would soon be back home.

One of the sergeants of the guard was an acquaintance of Renati and somehow, between the two, a large quantity of chocolate (about 50 boxes of Cadbury's milk bars) was brought into the camp and deposited in Renati's tent for sale to the prisoners. News of the chocolate's arrival was greeted enthusiastically by the men who were constantly hungry. But then the bombshell was dropped. The chocolate was for sale at two shillings a bar. Two shillings for a tuppeny bar of chocolate! The profiteering bastard! Abuse and invective was poured on his head, but Renati was unmoved. His expenses had been great, he pleaded. Transportation was costly, and besides, the guards had to have their cut. Despite his protestations and the prisoners' hunger, very few bars of chocolate were sold.

At that time of the year there are not many hours of darkness in Scotland, but during those hours, dangerously defying the night's curfew, a small group of men crawled silently to Renati's tent, and swiftly and silently cut the supporting guy ropes. In the resulting tumult and confusion the entire stock of chocolate disappeared. Very curiously, despite the breaking of the curfew, the commotion was completely disregarded by the guards, and the next morning's ration of tea, bread and margarine was made much more enjoyable by the appearance of several bars of chocolate in each tent. Apart from the damage to his wallet, Renati got off with a few bruises enthusiastically given to him by one of the raiders. The consensus of opinion was that he was lucky not to have had his throat cut in the incident.

The time at Woodhouselea passed in a series of hot sunny days, and the beautiful summer weather compensated a little for the uncertainty of our future and our constant hunger, for the rations were never adequate. We lazed in the warm sun, scratched at our ten days accumulation of dirt, (since our arrest no proper washing facilities had ever been available), and we engaged in repetitive and fruitless speculation about our future. No newspapers were to be had in the camp. No one knew anything of the progress of the war, and the officers who inspected the camp daily were deaf to our incessant questions. Wild and ever-changing rumours as to our eventual destination spread through the tents.

One day a fleet of buses drew up unannounced outside the barbed wire and a wave of excitement ran through the civilian prisoners at the sight of the passengers. Our relatives had finally been given news of our whereabouts and the authorities had laid on transportation for a visit. There were many touching scenes as relatives spoke to one another through the barbed wire. After days of uncertainty and worry, father spoke to son, brother to brother and wife to husband through the fence, for the arrests had created inexplicable anomalies. In many families a father had been arrested and a son left free, or a son taken and father left untouched. In others brother had been separated from brother, and the original 'Collar the lot' directive had been strangely implemented, for the arrests seemed to have been mostly of obviously harmless persons rather than of those who possibly merited internment.

On the outside, still at freedom, there were many known Fascist sympathisers, whilst inside the wire languished some who should never have been arrested on the night of June 10. Indeed, it became a standing joke to say that the only sure way to obtain your release was to apply for membership of the Fascist party! Much of the unfairness of that night was condensed into one incident. Sergeant Santangeli of the Highland Light Infantry had just arrived back in Glasgow for reassignment after two weeks bitter fighting in France against the advancing Germans, and had come close to death on the Dunkirk beaches. He stood staring in disbelief across the barbed wire at his elderly father who stood weeping, unkempt and unshaven, crying with joy at the sight of his soldier son. With a wild string of curses he tore off his uniform and ripped it to shreds on the barbed wire, tugging and tearing at the fence in helpless rage until he was dragged away by his comrades. His father, who should never have been arrested in the first place, was released from internment on the Isle of Man about two months later.

I too was overjoyed to see my father step down from one of the buses. We clasped hands through the fence as I tried to assure him that all was well with me and to tell mother not to worry on my behalf. I learned that my brother Ralph had received his call-up papers from the army and was reporting for duty that very day and that our ruined shop was still boarded up. A lawyer had been briefed to take up my case with the Home Office and the family was certain that I would soon be home.

On the morning of the eighth day at Woodhouselea we were made to gather our belongings. We were assembled in two groups, with married men on one side and sailors and single men on the other. With the division completed, I found myself in a group of merchant seamen and young men like myself. Until now very little contact had been made with the sailors, who had eyed the civilians with suspicion and reserve.

Who were these so-called Italians, some of whom spoke only English, some of whom spoke Italian only if forced to do so, and some who spoke freely with the guards in English? And the civilians looked askance at their strangely dressed companions with their almost incomprehensible accents and dialects. No explanation for the separation of the groups was given, so in order to stay with friends and relatives, many men simply lied with their feet. Married men professed to be single, and single men, married. Such simple acts can lead to dire consequences. What none of us knew at the time was that the married men were to be taken to the Isle of Man for a reasonably comfortable and uneventful internment, whilst the single men, many of them boys in their teens, were to be shipped thousands of miles away, some to meet death en route.

5
Warth Mills

Warth Mills, Bury, Lancashire was a disintegrating relic of the Industrial Revolution. Built in the early 19th century to meet the demands of the developing cotton trade, the mill had long fallen into disuse and had lain dank and derelict during the long depression of the 1930s. Stripped of its machinery, the stone floor was greasy and oily with disintegrating cotton rags everywhere. A fine dust hung in the air. There was no electricity: the only illumination was the daylight which filtered through the dirty cracked windows and glass panels which formed part of the roof.

The mill encompassed about two acres in area, and into this Dickensian scene were packed about 3,000 internees. The stench was well nigh unbearable. The original lavatory facilities, blackened and stained by long years of disuse, were inadequate and had been augmented by hastily dug latrines. Forty cold-water taps were available to meet the needs of the prisoners and the simple act of washing one's hands required long periods of queuing.

A double fence of barbed wire about seven feet high, constantly patrolled by armed guards, had been erected around the perimeter and hundreds of men stood, sat or squatted as near to it as possible, preferring the open air to the squalor of the interior. At least the camp at Woodhouselea had provided a clean environment with plenty of fresh air, but at Warth Mills it was as though the portals of Dante's inferno had opened up. The sights, sounds and smells were dreadful.

On arrival each prisoner was issued with a mattress and a blanket and made his bed wherever a piece of vacant dry ground could be found. Sleep was impossible amidst the coughing, moaning and weeping whilst in the pitch darkness of night the squeaking and scampering of rats added a further dimension of terror.

During the day fights would frequently break out over the sharing of rations and water facilities, and the old and infirm had to rely on the kindness and help of the young for their necessities. The place had been chosen as a transit area because of its proximity to Liverpool, which was to be the final embarkation point for the internees. At the time of the arrival of the Woodhouselea contingent, the inhabitants of the camp consisted of German and Italian internees and Jewish refugees fleeing the advance of Hitler's armies. All age groups were represented, from a boy of 15, named Arturo Vivante, to elderly men well into their seventies, for whom, lacking the resilience and adaptability of youth, the conditions must have been absolutely unbearable.

The commandant of the camp was Major Baybrook, who seemed a humane enough man, but all his attempts to ameliorate conditions were hopeless. Each day he would address the new arrivals, assuring them that all this was purely temporary, that soon they would be leaving for new destinations and that everyone should cooperate fully both with the authorities and with one another.

He listened sympathetically to all complaints and as the result of the protests of three Italian doctors there, some space was set aside for the elderly and the ill. Each morning a list was read out for that day's departure and the sound of their names would be greeted with relief by the lucky ones chosen. Everyone wanted to be out of the dreadful place, but I had to wait for a whole week until I heard my name called. That morning the departure list was read out by Captain Vinden, an officer who was to remain with our group for some months, and who came to figure prominently in future events.

The captain was a man of about 40, heavily built and with a slight limping gait, which was the result of a wound suffered during service on the Italian front during the 1914-18 war. He was brusque and ill tempered, spoke fluent Italian and seemed to be in the grip of a barely concealed dislike of Italians. The names read out that day were mainly Italian, with my own among them.

The train journey into the Liverpool dock area did not take long. The carriages drew into a dockside loading area, and as we stepped down we were made to walk a short distance onto a long quay to join groups of prisoners already assembled there. Running the length of the pier and towering over the loading sheds, a large, dull, grey ship lay at anchor. We faced the stern of vessel and on the rear deck, above the name *Arandora Star,* I could see what seemed to be coils of wire with the outline of a large gun behind them. I looked anxiously around me. Packed tightly on the quayside were thousands of men lined up the full length of the ship, some standing, some squatting and leaning against each other, some young, some old, and all with an apathetic resigned look about them. Rows of armed soldiers stood guard around us. After what seemed to be an interminable time, the crowd stirred slowly in answer to orders and began moving onto a gangway leading up to the ship, urged on by the soldiers. The loading of the ship proved to be a slow and lengthy process, but when the group ahead of me was reduced to about 200 men, the gangway was withdrawn.

By this time our group had been joined by hundreds upon hundreds of other prisoners. Most were civilians, but many of the newly arrived contingent wore military uniforms which immediately identified them as German soldiers. Some were in Luftwaffe uniform, some wore the dark blue outfits of marine commandos and all looked tired and weary. Most seemed unhurt, but some who wore bandages seemed incapable of standing upright and sat on the ground, leaning against the legs of their compatriots. We learned subsequently that there were 900 of them. Some were Luftwaffe personnel shot down over Southern England and France, with the majority of them marines captured at the time of the British raids on Stavanger and Narvik in Norway.

So we sat and stood and waited and watched as the *Arandora Star* drew away, and wondered what our fate was to be. We had not eaten since we had left Warth Mills that morning, and the pangs of hunger and thirst added to our general misery. Some time later another ship was manoeuvred alongside the quay. This ship bore the name *Ettrick* and seemed to be somewhat smaller, but it too was painted a dull grey, had coils of wire visible on the deck, and had a gun mounted at the stern as well. Again a gangway was run up to the deck, and orders to move up were issued. An army lorry was stationed at the entrance to the gangway, and as we shuffled past each of us was thrown a paper bag, which was full of hard-tack biscuits. The group from Warth Mills had remained intact, and as I moved up the gangway I looked behind to see that we would be followed by the German PoWs. The deck area seemed to be completely sealed off with barbed wire, behind which stood members of the crew curiously watching the proceedings. But we had little time to examine our surroundings, for no sooner had we taken a few steps along the deck, than we were made to descent into the bowels of the ship, urged on by a choleric little sergeant who stood at the top of a flight of stairs shouting abuse as we passed by.

The accommodation in which we found ourselves was small and cramped, and consisted of four large hold-like areas connected by a narrow passage. The space was completely devoid of furnishings and afforded barely enough space for everyone to lie down at the same time. A row of portholes on one side was sealed up and the sole illumination consisted of a few bulkhead lights high on the ceiling. Ventilation was through gratings on the wall and although the place seemed clean enough, the space available was totally inadequate for the 400 men crammed in there.

Two armed soldiers stood guard at the entrance and suddenly between them appeared the figure of Captain Vinden. A hush settled on the prisoners as he started to speak. He was not able to disclose our destination, he said, but could tell us that the journey would not be a long one and that the guards would be withdrawn from the door as soon as the ship sailed. The prisoners could then go freely up to the deck for fresh air. A barrage of questions went ignored, the Captain withdrew and we settled down as comfortably as we could, for we were by then experts in making the best of a bad situation.

At 6am the next morning the *Ettrick* set sail. As soon as she left the dock the guards were withdrawn and a group of us hurried out on deck. The implication of what we saw there did not immediately sink in. A section of the deck about 20 feet long and a few feet wide had been caged off with barbed wire which stretched from the deck to the roof above it, and sealed off the area completely. This left a passage to the section which contained the German PoWs, some of whom were already on deck. A barbed wire gate to the free deck was heavily padlocked and was guarded on the outside by two armed soldiers, while from the other side of the wire a handful of crew members stared curiously at the caged prisoners. The two groups of prisoners, Italian internees in one hold and the German PoWs in the other, nearly a thousand men all told, were effectively sealed off from the rest of the ship, with a heavily padlocked wire gate as the only point of exit in the event of an emergency.

6
The Ettrick

The *Arandora Star* had left Liverpool about 24 hours before us on the afternoon of the July 1 and had taken a route which had brought her north past the Isle of Man, through the North Channel between the Mull of Kintyre and Northern Ireland, past Malin Head, then due west into the open Atlantic. At approximately 1.30am on July 2, Gunther Prien, German U-boat commander, caught sight of the vessel in his periscope. Prien was the same commander who, on October 14, 1939, during the very first weeks of the war, had breached the supposedly impregnable defences at Scapa Flow, Orkney, to sink the battleship *Royal Oak*.

As his log book later showed, he was returning to base from a tour of duty in the North Atlantic, with just one torpedo remaining in the boat's arsenal. His instruments had alerted him to the presence of a ship in his vicinity and as he surveyed the *Arandora Star* through his periscope, he noted that the unmarked British vessel carried armaments fore and aft. He launched his last torpedo at her.

It struck in the boiler-room area in the aft region of the ship and within 30 minutes the *Arandora Star* sank to the bottom of the sea, taking about 720 souls with her. The full extent of the losses will never be known because the haphazard method of loading did not make for accuracy of count. The records show that she was carrying 1600 persons on board of which 374 were British, made up of soldiers and crew, 478 were German, consisting of the crews of two captured merchant ships, German nationals living in Britain and German-Jewish refugees. Seven hundred and twelve were Italians, all civilians living in the UK and broadly representative of the Italian immigrants there. The official casualty list showed that 486 Italians, 156 Germans and 79 Britons died.

ISLE OF THE DISPLACED

To the prisoners on the *Ettrick* the peril of our situation was only too apparent. Imprisoned as we were in the hold behind the fences of barbed wire, in the event of an emergency we would be caught in a trap and perish without the slightest hope of escape. Captain Vinden's promise that it would not be a long journey was our only consolation. Perhaps the Isle of Man was indeed our destination and if so our confinement would last for only a few hours.

I decided to stay for as long as possible on the deck area as I had no desire to go back into the cramped and badly-lit hold. At least I could breathe some fresh air. The soldiers on the other side of the wire seemed to have a friendly enough aspect, so I attempted a conversation with them. At the sound of my Scottish accent they responded freely enough, and expressed amazement at the nationality of their prisoners. They had been told that the men behind the wire were German PoWs and to be extremely careful when approaching them. Names and places of origin were exchanged. One of the soldiers hailed from Glasgow, knew our shop well and he promised me that on his return to Scotland he would get in touch with my parents with news of my whereabouts. Years later I was to learn that the soldier had indeed kept his promise, much to the relief of my parents. The news of the sinking of the *Arandora Star* with heavy internee casualties had been released in the UK to the consternation of every Italian family who thought that their relatives might have been on board that ship.

A chance remark from one of the guards revealed that the ship's destination was Canada and not the Isle of Man, as had been generally supposed. The information spread like wildfire through the prisoners, creating panic amongst us. To cross the Atlantic under such conditions, caged in like so many animals? How long would the journey take? It was just not possible, and many of the prisoners refused to believe the guard's remarks, repeating Captain Vinden's comment about a short journey. As the hours passed however, it became plain that the Isle of Man was being left far behind and the realisation that Canada was the destination set in.

Fortunately no one on board then knew the fate that had befallen the *Arandora Star* some hours before. As it was, the fear of an Atlantic crossing and the prospect of some unknown fate in far-off Canada only increased the misery of the men packed into the claustrophobic confines of the hold. Had the *Ettrick* been torpedoed and sunk there is no question that all the prisoners on board would have gone down with her, given the manner of their confinement. The ship was crammed to overflowing with a total of 3,500 men. Of these, 385 comprised the British crew and soldiers, commanded by Captain Howell. The prisoners consisted of 900 German PoWs of all ranks, about 1,800 Jewish refugees and German civilians and 407 Italians, 257 of them civilians and 150 merchant seamen. There were more men on the *Ettrick* than on the *Arandora Star*, a far bigger ship. The *Ettrick*, however, was a troop carrier and was designed to accommodate 2,800 men, though not in conditions such as we experienced. The presence of 900 highly-trained German soldiers who might have been a threat to crew and guards was probably the reason for the proliferation of barbed wire. The fact remains that the *Ettrick* was nothing less than a potential floating coffin.

The rumours persisted but on the second day at sea Captain Vinden confirmed that our destination was Canada. However, the leaked information from soldier to prisoner had a serious consequence for us. The free deck area next to the prisoners' cage was declared out of bounds to soldiers and crew alike, much to the regret of the prisoners who thereby lost a good source of cigarettes and information.

The news that Canada was indeed to be our destination cast a pall of gloom over us. The only ones happy at the prospect of landing in Canada were members of the Jewish groups on board. Although not actively persecuted as the German Jews had been, Italian Jews had suffered under the impact of the Fascist race laws of 1939, under which no Jew could hold government office, practise medicine or law, or follow the teaching professions.

Now, faced with what they thought was the certainty of a Nazi victory and consequently a Hitler-dominated Britain and Europe, the Italian Jews on board were glad to be leaving a continent which promised only the prospect of more persecution and suffering. The hundreds of German and Austrian Jews on board were doubly happy at the thought of Canada, for these refugees had known the terrors of Nazi persecution at first hand. But for the internees resident in Britain, exile to Canada meant separation from families and loved ones, because in the event of an Axis victory, which at that moment seemed probable, they worried that they might never again see their homes and families.

There was one Jew amongst them however who refused to

believe the story about our Canadian destination. Roberto Tagiuri was a young lawyer specialising in international law and he spent his days proclaiming to all and sundry, including a stone-faced Captain Vinden when available, that the transportation of civilian internees across war zones where they could be at risk, was illegal. It was just not conceivable that Britain could be in violation of the law and therefore Canada could not possibly be our destination!

Three weeks and more had now gone by since our internment. In that time we had been cut off from all news of the war. Wave upon wave of rumour swept through the prisoners and grew wilder as they spread. The almost unanimous feeling was that now France had fallen, Britain could not hold out against the Axis powers. The non-Jewish civilians were acutely worried that if the war were to end in a matter of weeks, they might find it difficult, if not impossible, to return home.

The weather, which had been warm and sunny for weeks, now worsened. The wind rose to gale force and the heavy seas brought the added misery of seasickness. There was hardly a man unaffected by the heaving motion of the ship and the smell of vomit and sickness lay heavy in the cramped confines of the hold. The inadequate flow of air through the ventilation ducts did little to dispel the laden atmosphere. The bad weather brought one benefit: it made us forget our constant yearning for proper food. Our rations each day consisted solely of bully beef and hard biscuits, masses of which were dumped each morning at the wire gate for distribution amongst us. No eating utensils were provided, apart from a tin mug for each man which could be filled at will from large tea urns set with their spouts inside the wire. One prisoner with some medical knowledge was heard to wonder how long it would be before we developed scurvy on such a diet!

The stormy weather lasted for two days, and the misery of the seasickness also served to dull the news of our Canadian destination. Once the men were able to move around more or less normally, a rota of sorts was established to give everyone a chance of going on deck to breathe some fresh air and to see some daylight.

An important difference between PoWs and civilian internees was that the latter had never been subjected to military discipline. Some of them did not take kindly to being told what to do in circumstances which required obedience and cooperation, and the group in the hold of the *Ettrick* at times proved difficult to handle. The sailors obeyed the commands of their officers quickly enough, but some of the civilians were reluctant to obey requests even if for the common good. In such cases force had to be applied, and this was done by volunteers with the necessary physical attributes.

Many prisoners preferred not to make use of the deck rota, and sat instead apathetically in the dim confines of the hold, but the majority were only too anxious to stay on deck for as long as possible for fresh air. A few however had to be forcibly removed from the deck to give everyone an opportunity to get away from the claustrophobic hold. Although the *Ettrick* had been designed as a troop ship, with adequate toilet facilities in normal circumstances, the latrines had been unable to cope with a combination of overcrowding and seasickness. Buckets were provided for emergency use. When full, these had to be emptied over the side by the prisoners and because hours would sometimes pass before a guard was provided as escort, the smell was terrible. It was small wonder that some prisoners did all they could to spend more than their allotted time on deck.

We had thought that the conditions at Warth Mills were bad, but what we had to undergo on the *Ettrick* was infinitely worse. Ralph Taglione, a Londoner and manager of the Café Royal in Regent Street, had appointed himself as spokesman for the civilians. Merchant seaman Captain Bonorino acted for the sailors, and between them some semblance of order was imposed in the hold. But protests were made in vain to the guards about the conditions in the hold. On one occasion, Captain Bonorino, with me at his side as interpreter, insisted to a soldier that the captain be sent for. Vinden listened impassively as Bonorino ran off a long list of complaints in Italian, then answered roughly in the same language.

'*Fatela finita con questi pianti. Non lo sapete che siamo in guerra? Voi Italiani siete buoni soltanto per cantare e per chiavare.*'[1]

Even if this was an accurate statement, it hardly justified being kept in such appalling conditions.

He then turned brusquely and limped off. Bonorino shrugged stoically.

'*A quello qualche Italiano gli deve aver fatto le corna.*'[2]

---

[1] 'Have done with these complaints, don't you know that we are at war? You Italians are good only for singing and fucking.'
[2] 'Some Italian or other must have had it off with his wife.'

7
Division

On the seventh day at sea I was to have my first taste of Fascist rule by fear. On the walls of a toilet cubicle someone had scribbled the words:

Curse Mussolini and all who disturb the peace of the world.

The writing was in English, and when translated into Italian for the benefit of the sailors, their anger was aroused. One of them, Fernando Malusa, a radio officer, was a Fascist who made this the occasion for a vitriolic tirade against the anti-Fascists in their midst. To be anti-Fascist was to be anti-Italian, he raged. There were obviously traitors amongst us, and everyone should be on the alert for those who dared to speak out against *Il Duce*. To be against him was to be against Italy itself.

The litany continued. Watch and listen to your neighbour, he urged. Trust no stranger, and any who spread despondency and negative ideas should be reported immediately to him. He would keep a list of all such traitors, he promised, and they would be dealt with appropriately on the day of Italy's undoubted victory. Thus was born the dreaded *libretto nero*, the little black book of names, which was to grow considerably in size over the next few years. The black book was to ensure that all those who dared speak their mind or follow the courage of their convictions would be suitably punished after the Axis victory.

And so the prisoners began to form into mutually suspicious and antagonistic groups, the Fascists on one side, the Jews and a handful of Communists on the other. In the middle was the large majority who took no sides and who wished only to be free and reunited with their families.

These groups were separated at their extremes by the language problem. Among the civilian prisoners English was the main language in use. Most of the London-Italians spoke no Italian at all, neither did many of the Scots-Italians, and this language barrier sowed seeds of enmity and suspicion amongst the Italian sailors. Amongst them the word *Inglesi* was used to describe a section of their fellow prisoners rather than their captors.

The completely bilingual prisoners like myself, who were at home in both languages, were in the minority, and we faced the difficulty of understanding the strange and almost incomprehensible accents of some of the sailors. All these were factors which kept alight the embers of a mutual distrust and dislike which led to much friction in the years to come. To this simmering cauldron was added a political element. Amongst the internees there were some who had been actively opposed to Fascism. Two London-based Italians, Peter Bassani and Aldo Gatti had both fought in the International Brigade against Franco in the Spanish Civil War and freely made their opinions known. There were a handful more with strong left-wing views.

I suppose it might be true to say that for whatever reason I have always been a bit of a chameleon. No doubt my bilingual upbringing during the early years in Glasgow had much to do with it, but I always seem to have had the ability to mix and merge with persons of different nationalities and cultural backgrounds. Moreover I was quite gregarious, so I circulated as best I could in the hold amongst the prisoners, and engaged all and sundry in conversation. I soon realised what an interesting group of people my companions were, with the Jews obviously the intellectual cream of the lot.

In that group were Carlo Treves, lecturer in chemistry at Rome University, a small pleasant man who had been dismissed from his post when the Fascist anti-Semitic laws were passed. He had come to London as a refugee, hoping to find a use for his skills there. Emilio Barocas, assistant to the Astronomer Royal at Greenwich Observatory: he had been literally plucked from his telescope during the night by the police. There was Arturo Valente, the 15-year-old schoolboy son of a Nobel Prize winner, whose treatment later in the camp was to trigger off a nasty incident. Roberto Tagiuri, the law professor already mentioned, was to bore us all for months about the flouting of international law. Giorgio Randegger, a vitriolic left-wing journalist who was to be at perpetual loggerheads with the camp's Fascists. These formed part of a 25-strong group of Jewish refugees.

The Scots-Italians formed a strong group. There was Lawrence Crolla and his two brothers, Vincent and Michael, the three sons of a well-known Glasgow ice-cream family and Peter Nesti, a quiet and unobtrusive terrazzo worker; Dino Orsi, of the generous heart at Woodhouselea and Lawrence DiCiacca, a tall and likeable chap whom I used to meet frequently at the fish market. There was Joe Salotti from Prestwick and Angelo LaMarra from Bishopbriggs. A good friend was Joe Guidi from the Alhambra Restaurant in Argyle Street, Glasgow and prominent in the group was John Di Mambro, a thick-set, powerfully built lad not slow to stand up for his rights against anyone. From the Paisley area we had Dante Toti, a tall and imposing figure originally from Barga and like me, bilingual. His ability to mix freely with the sailors was later to help break down some of the barriers between the various factions among the prisoners.

The London area was well represented. Aldo Sampietro, head chef at the Savoy, was later to cook us some magnificent meals in the camp. There was Tino Moramarco, a tall, handsome gigolo and ex-Olympic athlete, scores of merchants and shopkeepers from Soho and a couple of taciturn East Enders, Tontini and Servignini, whose many scars spoke of battles with London gangs. Prominent in this group from England was Giorgio Martinez, a Cambridge educated youth from Naples, whose father Giuseppe was the founder of the Pirelli Cable Co in Southampton. Scotland was represented by a contingent of about 35, and huddled amongst us as if in a little group of their own, seeking protection from the rough company in which they found themselves, were three priests and three novices.

Padre Roffinella was a tall, ascetic-featured Jesuit who had been arrested at the Farm Street Jesuit Centre in London. We soon gave him the nickname *Torquemada*, since he reminded us of that painting from the time of the Spanish Inquisition which portrayed a man of similar appearance. Padre Schlisizzi, on a pastoral visit to the Italians of London at the time of his arrest, was a well-fleshed-out Roman priest whose ample girth and general manner spoke more of a taste for the earthly delights than of the penances of religion. Padre Frizzero was a pensive and devout Xavierian whose demeanour exemplified all the expected priestly qualities. The three novices, whose names I never could remember, were unobtrusive timid youths who spent the time clutching their rosaries, terrified of their situation and of the company in which they found themselves.

I was fascinated by these diverse types, as they were so different from the circles in which I moved in Glasgow. I was fascinated too by the merchant seamen in the group. They represented an Italy which I knew nothing about. Italy had been unified only about 60 years before, so these sailors came from regions in the south vastly different from my native Tuscany. A large percentage of them were completely illiterate, and some could speak only their own dialect. Nevertheless I moved freely amongst them too, and I like to think that in some small way I helped to ease the suspicion with which they regarded the civilians. The great benefit to me of all this was that it took my mind away from our desperate situation and helped to quicken the passage of the 12 days the journey was to last.

The case of Martinez senior is an interesting example of the indiscriminate nature of the application of government policy in the matter of the internment of Italians. At the beginning of the war with Germany some ten months before in 1939, the British merchant fleet had begun to suffer heavy losses because of the Germans' use of a new naval weapon, the magnetic mine. These sea mines were placed at undetectable depths in the busy sea lanes around the British coast and were detonated by the proximity of a magnetic field such as that generated by the mass of iron in the hull of a ship. This new weapon caused consternation at the Admiralty, for the losses sustained by Allied shipping could have paralysed Britain's only supply line.

To counter this threat the Pirelli boffins produced a solution: the degaussing cable. This was a thick wire cable placed under and around the hull of a ship. An electric current of determined strength was then passed through the cable, thus producing an electrical field which neutralised the magnetic field created by the metallic mass of the ship. As a result the magnetic mines below were rendered ineffective. Within a matter of weeks all Allied shipping was equipped with degaussing cables many of which were produced under the supervision of Giuseppe Martinez at his factory in Southampton. Despite this most important contribution to the war effort, within a matter of hours of Italy's declaration of war, and without interrogation or investigation, Giuseppe Martinez was arrested with his eldest son Carlo. After a stay at the dreadful Warth Mills camp he found himself together with several hundred other Italians on a dock at Liverpool slowly being loaded on the *Arandora Star*. The youngest son George remained at liberty for two more days, until he too was arrested and decanted on to the *Ettrick*.

Guiseppe and Carlo found themselves in cramped but fairly adequate quarters in a small single cabin deep in the bowels of the ship. No sooner had they set sail however, than they were ordered out of their cabin by an English officer, who presumably needed it for his own use. The only space they could find was a section of the upper deck which fortunately was not enveloped in barbed wire. From there they were blasted into the open sea by the impact of Gunther Prien's torpedo. For several hours they floated on the debris-covered sea, surrounded by the dead and dying, until rescued by a Canadian destroyer.

On July 9, together with hundreds of other survivors from the *Arandora Star,* they were marched onto another converted cruise ship, the *Dunera,* which docked two months later in Australia. The atrocious conditions aboard that ship have been well documented and were the subject of *Internment in Australia* written by Father Walter Konig of the Society of Jesuits, published in Melbourne in 1963. But the Martinez' extraordinary story did not stop there and others close to them were to have strange experiences as well. Shortly before the outbreak of the war with Italy, George had become engaged to Mariolina Antonucci, the daughter of a colonel in the Italian army. Shortly after her engagement she went to visit her father, who was in command of a unit stationed in Jimma, a small town some miles south-west of Addis Ababa in Ethiopia.

No sooner had she arrived than war broke out, and there she remained until the town was captured by the British on the April 6, 1941. The final defeat of the Italian Army at Keren some weeks later signalled the collapse of Italian resistance in Africa, and all Italian civilians in Ethiopia were rounded up and interned. Together with some others, Miss Antonucci was taken to an internment camp in Madera, an outpost in Somaliland, where she was stripped of all her personal jewellery and valuables. She had no knowledge of the fate of her fiancé George, nor he of her's. Indeed, the remaining Martinez family in Naples (George's mother and one other brother) were convinced that all the family had perished on the *Arandora Star*. It was not until almost a year after our arrival in Canada that the family were put in touch through the International Red Cross.

After several more months Miss Antonucci was repatriated and, overjoyed at the news of her fianc's survival, wrote him a letter with all her news. Incensed at hearing of Mariolina's treatment and loss, with the Camp Commandant's permission, George wrote to the Home Office in London stating the facts of the case. In due time he received a polite acknowledgement.

The war ended, George and Mariolina married and settled down in Romsey in the south of England, where he again took up his career. Some months later a neatly-packed parcel was delivered to them. Inside it and none the worse for wear, were all the valuables and jewels taken from Mariolina in Ethiopia in April 1941!

My curiosity also took me over to the PoW side of the deck (if the wire-enclosed passageway that connected our two holds could be called that). Communication was not easy. I spoke no German, and the few of them who had some words of English at first showed no inclination to fraternise. My fairly long conversations through the wire with the guards had been noted and I was looked upon with some diffidence, if not suspicion.

The PoWs were all young, fit and very disciplined. Their periods on deck were strictly controlled, unlike ours, and I had the impression that their organisation in the hold was not as haphazard as ours was. But then they were soldiers; we were not. I persisted with my attempts to make conversation with them, until Captain Bonorino suggested that they might regard me as a spy, upon which my wanderings to the German 'front' abruptly ceased.

8
Reception

On the morning of the July 15, twelve days after setting sail from Liverpool, a shout of excitement rang out from the deck. Land was sighted and with it came the prospect of an end to our misery. It animated even those most sunk in apathy and self-pity. What in fact had been sighted was the southern shore of Newfoundland and our journey was to last another day as the *Ettrick* moved slowly through the Cabot Straits, into the Gulf of St Lawrence, and then into the wide estuary of the river. On the morning of the 14th the ship docked at the city of Quebec and the prisoners were unloaded at the docks by the old citadel in the shadow of Chateau Frontenac.

Clutching our belongings, all 407 of us stumbled awkwardly down the gangplank. Those who had never moved from the confines of the hold were half-blinded by the unaccustomed sunlight, but those who could gazed around in wonder at our new surroundings. The scent of flowers and shrubs and fresh air was immediately appreciated by everyone. As we came down the gangplank, one by one, our names were taken by Captain Vinden, and we then assembled on the quayside which was tightly ringed by armed soldiers and military vehicles. We presented a sorry sight. For a month now we had lived and slept in the same clothes, and only the most rudimentary hygiene had been possible. Many had not shaved for weeks and as we stood in clothes stained with vomit and excrement, lice-ridden and scratching, a more unkempt and dirty bunch would have been hard to imagine.

We sat and waited on the dock for some time, looking at the magnificent vistas of Quebec around us. Then, in response to the orders of the captain, we began to shuffle out of the dock area

RECEPTION

through a gauntlet of soldiers. Orders were given in an almost incomprehensible English-French patois, the meaning of which was plain enough when accompanied by the butt end of a rifle. A huge Canadian Pacific train had got up steam by the dockside and we climbed into it as our suitcases and belongings were snatched away unceremoniously in the process. As we got on each man was issued with a large brown paper bag which, to our delight, contained a welcome and unexpected surprise. Inside was the whitest of white bread, cheese, fruit, tins of tuna fish, little pats of butter and miniature jars of jam and marmalade. Whoops of joy greeted the discovery, and elation spread contagiously throughout us. We reacted like children who had just been given surprise bags of sweets.

As we settled down to our new surroundings, Captain Vinden limped through the carriages, which were of an open type strange to our eyes. In each one he made a short statement to the effect that the food just issued had to last two days and thus was to be rationed accordingly. Then he disappeared, not to be seen again for two eventful days.

The train set off to the sound of song and merriment. Having eaten and enjoyed some of the food, for my appetite was now beginning to return, I settled back comfortably to enjoy the unfolding majesty of the Canadian scenery. The train puffed steadily through villages and hamlets with strange-sounding French names: Pont Rouge, Deshamboult, Trois Rivières, and as the day went on speculation mounted as to our possible destination. Night had fallen when the train drew up in what was obviously a large city, and the name Montreal spread rapidly through the carriages. A small fleet of buses and military vehicles had drawn up beside the train, and we were given orders to move out. It seemed we had finally arrived.

Holding on tightly to our precious food parcels, we began to file out of the carriages, laughing and joking amongst ourselves and shouting pleasantries at the impassive guards who stood with rifles and bayonets at the ready at the exit to each compartment. Chattering excitedly to my companions and holding my food parcel firmly, I jumped up the few steps onto one of the buses. In the back were three guards. When 20 men were loaded into each vehicle three more guards were positioned at the exit and the doors closed.

In all there were 20 buses, and all were being loaded in the same manner. The fleet of vehicles then moved off, preceded by some sort of military half-track with a machine-gun mounted on the rear. Glancing back, I could see a similar armoured car making up the rear of the convoy.

The vehicles made their way along the brightly-lit streets of the city, with policemen at each intersection ensuring an unhindered passage for the convoy. We carried on through quieter streets until we reached the massive spans of a huge steel girdered bridge. Looking down from aloft a cluster of intense bright lights under the far end of the bridge, a hundred yards or so away, caught my eye. The buses slowed to a crawl and I could see about 80 feet below us a small rectangular area flooded in the glare of powerful searchlights.

There were uniformed figures moving around in front of a long, low, building of some sort and as the buses reached the end of the bridge to begin a slow descent, the lights disappeared from view, leaving only a bright glow in the sky. Slowly the convoy moved on, and finally came to a halt in front of a set of iron gates flanked on either side by the pillars of a massive stone archway. The leading armoured car slowly preceded the first bus through the gates, followed by the second bus, then after a short interval, by the third.

It was then our turn, and the bus jerked forward and stopped after a few yards. A blinding light shone into the interior, the door flew open, the three guards at the front jumped out, and a blast of sound erupted into the bus.

'Heraus! Heraus! Schnell! Out!', and suddenly frightened, we descended from the bus, urged on by the three guards at the rear.

I paused at the top of the step, blinded by the dazzling light in my eyes. A hand reached out, grabbed the lapel of my jacket and pulled me sprawling to the ground. I tried to get up. Another set of hands pulled at my food parcel. Instinctively I held on and pulled back. A truncheon smashed into my forearm, forcing me to release my grip and I fell to my knees, impelled forward by a blow to my back. Dazed and shaken I was hauled to my feet by two soldiers shouting at me in German.

'Schnell! Schnell!'

I was dragged forward several steps, then with a rifle butt blow to my back, I was forced to the ground in a squatting position. This procedure was repeated as each unsuspecting prisoner stepped

RECEPTION

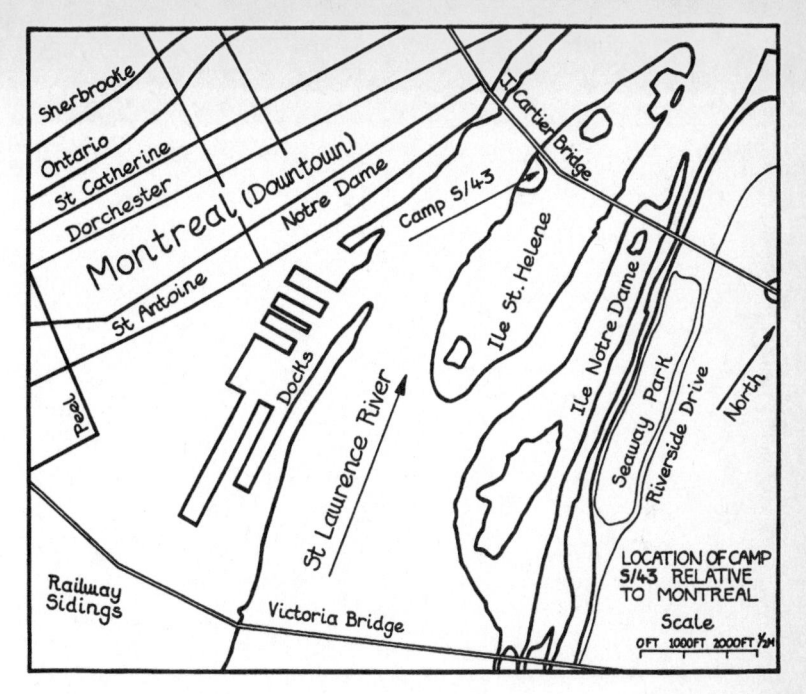

Map showing location of Camp S/43 relative to Montreal. Labels include: Sherbrooke, Ontario, St Catherine, Dorchester, St Antoine, Peel, Montreal (Downtown), Notre Dame, Camp S/43, Docks, St Lawrence River, Ile St. Helene, Jacques Cartier Bridge, Ile Notre Dame, Seaway Park, Riverside Drive, North, Railway Sidings, Victoria Bridge. Scale: 0FT 1000FT 2000FT ½M

down. Some fared better than others, but everyone had their food parcels clubbed from them and all of were pushed, butted, and kicked to a squatting position on the ground while the guards continued their verbal tirade. The priests fared worse of all, for the sight of their habit seemed to spur the guards to even greater effort, and the six unfortunates were clubbed and kicked unmercifully, their clothes all but torn from their backs.

As each bus entered, the focus of attention was drawn further away from our group and I sat rigid with fear, trying to summon up enough courage to inconspicuously angle my head slightly to observe our surroundings. There were three groups of prisoners before ours already sitting on the ground, each with four soldiers standing over them menacingly. Clearly each group had been greeted in the same way as ours, for they were all bruised, their clothes torn and bloodstained.

We were sitting in some kind of courtyard, and as my eyes became accustomed to the glare of the searchlights I made out the outline of the long, low, building in the background. Curious as I was to see behind me, I did not dare move my head for fear of another blow, but from the corner of my eye I could make out a high

ISLE OF THE DISPLACED

wooden platform. On it was a machine-gun manned by a soldier. My stomach grew cold with fear. Armed soldiers paraded up and down in front of us, and paused occasionally to fire shots into the air. Half a dozen huge Alsatian dogs roamed in and out of the squatting men, sniffing and barking furiously and adding to the general air of intimidation. If all this had been meant to cow and frighten, then the plan had succeeded very well indeed, for we sat petrified with terror, and the thought passed through my mind that this could very well be our last moment on earth.

Some in the group were crying quietly, some were repeating Hail Marys under their breath, some were cursing quietly. Jimmy Berretti, a tall quiet youngster from Ayr was shivering uncontrollably despite the warmth of the night, and I could feel nausea and panic begin to well up inside me. Sitting cross-legged in front of me was Aldo Girasole, my cellmate at the time of my arrest. One of the marauding dogs stopped beside him and peed on his leg. 'Fuckin' bastards. . . fuckin' bastards!' was his angry whisper at which my growing panic turned into a semi-hysterical giggle.

Yet even in such moments a sense of humour can show itself. Aldo Magris, headwaiter from Quaglino's famous London restaurant, sat massaging a painful spot on his ribs where a rifle butt had struck. In the area of the blow he discovered a long forgotten pocket, from which he surreptitiously extracted a packet of condoms. Glancing around carefully to be sure of escaping detection, he proceeded to blow one up, gave it a sharp tap, and the resulting balloon floated gently up into the warm night air. This was followed by two more, until Aldo was discovered and given a sore head as well.

The unloading and manhandling took the better part of two hours and when completed we were in 20 groups of 20 frightened men sitting on the ground, fearfully and passively awaiting whatever else might be in store for us. A Canadian officer approached the first group and began to shout at them in a staccato flow of German. Enraged at the lack of response, he repeated himself even louder, and poked his stick at one of the prisoners in front of him. Ralph Taglione, one side of his face badly swollen from a blow, raised a hesitant hand and spoke in a cultivated English accent.

'Please sir. . . nobody here speaks German'.

The officer looked at him blankly. 'What do you mean you don't speak German? What bloody language do you speak?'

RECEPTION

'Please sir, everybody here speaks English'.

'English?', the officer seemed confused. 'What do you mean English? Where do you come from?'

'Please sir, in this group we are all Italians from London'.

The officers jaw sagged slightly. He looked oddly at Taglione, then turned on his heels to confer with a major standing close by. The major motioned to Taglione who stood up and hobbled over to the him, barely able to walk. He questioned Taglione closely, and I could see him listening intently to the Londoner's answers. These were long and fluent, punctuated by a series of gestures, ending with a characteristic arms half-raised, palms upturned, hunched shoulders pose which spoke volumes.

It will probably never be possible to discover the combination of events which brought 407 Italian internees to a camp obviously prepared for high-risk Nazis and the truth of the matter will probably remain unknown forever to those who suffered that night. Was the sinking of the *Arandora Star* a factor? Had the camp been prepared for the Germans who sailed on *that* ship? But the Germans on the *Arandora Star* were all Jewish or political refugees who no more merited the treatment of that first night than we Italians did. Were the priests singled out for special treatment because it was thought that they were spies disguised as priests? Why were the soldiers' commands given in German? Why were all the notices in the compound written in that language? The camp had obviously been specifically prepared for an intake of high-risk German PoWs such as the *Ettrick* had carried. Could there have been a mix up at Quebec, with our group sent off to the wrong destination?

But Captain Vinden knew the truth about the men whose names he had read out in Warth Mills some two weeks before. He certainly knew their nationality, so why had the colonel in charge of the reception of the prisoners who was obviously convinced that he was dealing with Germans, not been informed of their true identity?

What is certain is that no one, least of all a bunch of hapless internees consisting of boys, old men, shopkeepers, waiters, chefs, doctors, refugees and deckhands should have been subjected to the calculated brutalities of that night. And all for having committed the crime of being born an Italian or possessing an Italian name. That no one was killed or seriously injured is remarkable, and the memory of the first night at Camp S will long remain in the minds of those who experienced it.

After the questioning of Taglione the attitude of the soldiers changed dramatically. Orders were now given in English, and although the voices were as rough as before, no more blows were delivered and the marauding dogs were withdrawn from the compound. The first group of men was made to strip off their clothes, then ordered into a dimly-lit room with two rows of showers. Before entering the showers, all body hair was sheared off by a group of soldiers wielding electric hair clippers, then, issued with a bar of soap, each man was ordered into the showers. Hot and heavily-disinfected water streamed out of the first row and then after a cold rinse in the second row, the first group of men were paraded dripping wet in front of a bored medical officer. From a safe distance behind a plain wooden table, his examination consisted of a prod with a swagger stick and a quick glance at the front and back of each prisoner. Although all use of excessive force had stopped we were still being manhandled and the soldiers emphasised their verbal commands with shoves and pushes.

As I was in the fourth group waiting to be stripped, shorn, showered and examined I had ample time to notice that as each man undressed, all pockets were emptied out and rings, bracelets, watches, pens and anything of any value was confiscated by the guards. A Scots-Italian in our group, Peter Nesti, had a small mother-of-pearl fountain pen in his pocket. When he saw what was happening, he hid it by surreptitiously inserting it into his anus as he squatted on the ground. I wore a gold crucifix ring of a type fashionable in those days in Glasgow-Italian families and which had been given to me many years before by my mother. This had great sentimental value for me, and I had no wish for it to be stolen. I flattened the ring as best I could and placed it between my toes, where it remained safely hidden during the shearing and washing procedures. George Martinez wore a handsome gold ring gifted to him a few months before in Naples by his newly-acquired fiancée. He saved this by tying it into the sleeve of his shirt before being stripped and searched, then popping it into his mouth before throwing his discarded clothes into the growing heap. (For many days afterwards gleeful prisoners exchanged stories about the various ways in which they had managed to save cherished objects.

My birthplace, Bacchionero, in the hills above Barga, as it is now.

My grandfather, Francesco as he was in 1920 at about the age of 95. He died in 1927.

My parents, Francesco and Maria in 1909, around the time of their marriage before emigration to the United States.

My mother with my brother Ralph outside the tenement in St Paul, Minnesota, 1912.

My father (centre) and four other sergeants in uniform during the Libyan campaign, 1912.

My father on arrival in Glasgow, 1919.

The hilltop town of Barga, Tuscany.

The family café on the corner of Renfrew St and Hope St, Glasgow. It was from above the café that I watched the looting of the premises on June 10, 1940. The Savoy was demolished in 1971.

My alien's registration book, issued in 1940. It was rescinded in 1960.

The entrance to the camp, Ile Sainte Hélène, Montreal, in the 1970s.

The main frontage of the camp building. There was no ivy in the 1940s and the grounds were somewhat less manicured!

Cartoon drawn by one of the Afrika Korps PoWs captioned *Die Rundendreher*, referring to the boring daily grind of circling the camp square for exercise.

Die Rundendreher

Printed by War Prisoners' Aid, Y.M.C.A.

A group of UK-Italians in 1943 prior to my release. The author is standing to the left. To his left is Lawrence Crolla of Glasgow. Michael Crolla (now dead) stands in the back row, right. On his right, with his arm around Michael's shoulder is George Barletta, the man who escaped to bicycle around Montreal! Seated, second from the left is Osvaldo Pelosi from Wales and on his left, Vincent Crolla, brother of Lawrence and Michael, now also dead.

O'Connor Lynch, the camp censor/interpreter in the years just after the war.

George Martinez, graduating from Cambridge, a few months prior to the outbreak of war.

The author at the entrance to the camp in the 1970s.

RECEPTION

These tales, sometimes embellished, raised morale amongst the men. In our situation such little acts of defiance could be considered victories against our captors).

It was soon my turn to undergo the cleaning procedure. I was quickly rid of a month's accumulation of grime and dirt, after which I was issued with a large towel and a bundle of clothes. Vastly relieved that orders were now being given less forcefully, I followed the shouted instructions of the guards and ran up some wooden steps into a long, low and dimly-lit vaulted room. The only furnishings were two rows of double-tiered metal bunks, separated by a passage no more than three feet wide, and each supplied with a mattress and folded blankets. A sergeant stood by, directing each of us to a bunk and, barely dry, utterly drained and exhausted by the events of the day, I fell instantly asleep.

9
Ile Sainte Hélène

The next morning dawned to a completely changed atmosphere in the camp. As we woke up and cautiously poked our faces out of the dormitories, no military presence was to be seen, and soon the compound was full of men taking in the details of our new accommodation.

A long three-sided building of three floors, surmounted by a gently sloping roof, the structure was made of stone blocks about two feet thick. Access to the ground floor was by means of two large doors in the centre section, whilst the upper floors could be reached both by internal wooden stairs and from the outside by means of sets of stone steps leading directly up from the compound. The floors of the upper sections were of rough wood, and the ground floor was paved with large flagstones. The rear of the fortress was an unbroken stone wall and at the front of the building, regularly spaced window apertures gave light and ventilation.

Across the front of the building a seven-foot-high, double barbed-wire fence had been erected to form a courtyard about 100ft wide by 350ft long. At either end of the fence stood an elevated wooden tower, each equipped with a heavy machine-gun manned by three soldiers. The whole structure ran parallel to the river, separated from it by some 50 yards of gently sloping ground. Across the river lay the city of Montreal, surmounted by a huge neon illuminated crucifix on the heights of Mount Royal beyond. Dominating the scene was the impressive structure of the Jacques Cartier bridge as it passed over the northern end of the building, with one of its giant concrete pylons almost touching the perimeter fence of the compound. The old fortress of Ste Hélène, built so many years ago by Champlain on the island named after his young bride, was now serving as an internment camp for 407 Italian prisoners.

News of the arrival of the prisoners had evidently filtered through to the population of Montreal, for the bridge was thronged with curiosity seekers strolling along the walkway, stopping whenever possible to stare at the packed compound below them. Soldiers posted on the bridge kept the pedestrians on the move. These soldiers, together with the machine-gun crews on the towers, were the only military personnel in sight.

The men had now donned the clothes given to them the night before, which consisted of a blue shirt with a large red circle on

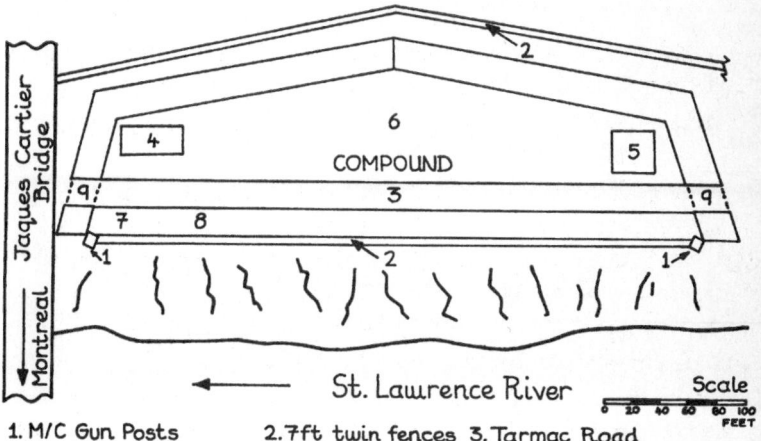

1. M/C Gun Posts   2. 7ft twin fences 3. Tarmac Road
4. Red X Bandage Shop 5. Recreation Hut 6. Football Area (summer)
7. Singsong Area (summer) 8. Ice Rink (Winter) 9. Entrances 2 steel gates

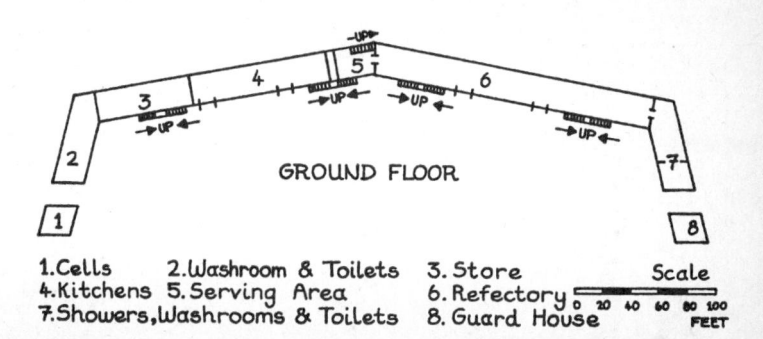

1. Cells   2. Washroom & Toilets   3. Store
4. Kitchens   5. Serving Area   6. Refectory
7. Showers, Washrooms & Toilets   8. Guard House

the back, trousers with a broad red stripe running down the side of the leg, and a blue jacket, also with a large red circle on the back. As the morning wore on without any sign of guards appearing inside the compound, the men gained confidence, and soon the courtyard was packed with a milling mass of blue-clad prisoners. Although the space available was very limited, after the claustrophobia of the *Ettrick* the men revelled in the luxury of freedom of movement, and strolled around exchanging experiences of the night before, comparing cuts and bruises.

After some time the gates of the camp swung open to signal the entrance of a group of soldiers. The officer who interrogated Ralph Taglione the night before, stepped forward and began to address us from the top of the stone steps set into the wall of the fortress. With a slight Irish intonation to his voice, he introduced himself as Major O'Donohoe, the Camp Commandant, and with no reference to the events of the night before, informed us that this was to be our permanent camp. He then presented to us Captain Pitblado, who was to instruct us in the routine of the camp.

The captain was a jolly looking, rotund little man approaching middle age, with the face and manner of an avuncular WC Fields. He smiled broadly, waved a hand as if in greeting, then proceeded to address the assembled prisoners in the manner of a boy scout leader exhorting his adolescent charges.

This was to be our home for the foreseeable future, he said, so everyone had to cooperate to make it comfortable for all. Each group of 20 had now to choose a leader, who in turn would elect a Camp Leader, who would be in daily contact with the military to ensure the smooth running of the camp. Provisions would now be arriving, and the first task of the prisoners would be the selection of their own kitchen personnel. He beamed cheerfully at us and gave a little wave with a plump hand. He then concluded his address with a little homily by which he was to be forever remembered, and which was to become the catch phrase of the camp.

'Now lads, now that we know one another we've got to play ball together. You play ball with me and I'll play ball with you'.

At this, there were a number of understandable *sotto voce* comments from the prisoners, still nursing the bruises of the night before. Then, flanked by two massively built sergeants, Le Seour and Rutherford, the former of whom had been noticed acting with great enthusiasm and vigour at the reception of the previous night, the little captain began a tour of the compound. He nodded pleasantly to all and sundry; his manner that of a paternal schoolmaster making himself acquainted with his pupils. He stopped from time to time to speak to individual prisoners, always finishing the conversation with his catchphrase. . . 'You play ball with me and I'll play ball with you'.

Nevertheless, Pitblado's manner and walkabout amongst the prisoners served the purpose of creating a much more relaxed and less fearful atmosphere in the camp. Moreover the promise of the arrival of provisions and the prospect of good and regular meals boosted morale, pushing into the background the memory of the brutalities of the previous night. Captain Vinden then made an appearance at the top of the steps. He had spoken no more than a few words when the men showed one of the very few examples of solidarity in the face of their captors. A low and sustained sound of booing arose from the compound and the prisoners retreated into the interior of the building, leaving the captain to direct his words to an empty courtyard. There was no questioning the unanimity of feeling as to the captain's role, or lack of it, in the previous night's proceedings. After a few more weeks of occasional appearances in the camp he was never seen again.

The first few days in the camp passed in a flurry of organisational activity. We were such a disparate group of individuals from so many different backgrounds that the organisation of the camp was not an easy matter. We did not even share a common language. A good 20 per cent of the men spoke only English, and many of the sailors spoke only their own dialects. Apart from the sailors none of us had ever been subjected to any form of group discipline. It has been said that in any group of four Italians you will find five different opinions on any given subject. The proof of such an observation could be found in the behaviour of the Camp S inmates in the simple matter of choosing group leaders for themselves. No people on earth have been as well conditioned by experience and history to be suspicious and cynical of those placed in authority over them as the Italians, and this dislike of authority is often transformed into lack of cooperation and civil disobedience.

Therefore the act of picking one person from a group of 20 strangers to be their representative became a labour of monumental proportions. Many, ever suspicious of motives, changed their minds from one moment to another; for to put power, however little, into the hands of an individual until one could be sure of that person's patronage, became a matter of the utmost importance.

Amongst the merchant seamen these matters were quickly resolved, for they already had a chain of command which they continued to adhere to. In some of the groups the background of origins was so similar, as in ours, for example, where all the prisoners came mainly from a Scottish environment, that the selection of a leader was not a matter of great argument. In some of the other groups however, the problem was not so easily resolved.

Not only did the members of these groups come from a great variety of social backgrounds, but it has to be remembered that Italy at that time had become a nation only a few decades before. Despite Mussolini's furious efforts to instil a sense of nationhood, there remained a vast and almost unbridgeable gulf between the northern and southern regions of the country. There was, and to some extent there is still to this day, a great division between the cultural and psychological background of a Milanese or a Tuscan, and that of a Calabrian or a Sicilian. Add to this quasi racial difference the political elements in the camp, with Fascists, Communists and Liberals scattered throughout, and one had a perfect recipe for disorder.

In time, however, the question of group leaders and then of camp leadership was settled. The function of the Camp Leader was to liaise with the military authorities and for this role Tino Moramarco was chosen. He was a tall and handsome figure of a man, about six foot tall, of magnificent physique, and had formed part of the Italian decathlon team in the 1936 Berlin Olympics, although without any great success. His present occupation was obscure. The unkind ones in the camp said that he was nothing but a gigolo, but whatever his occupation, he cut an imposing figure at the head of the camp. Since he was not possessed of any great intellect and did as he was told by his companions, he was reckoned to be just right for the job.

The first item to be sorted out was the staffing of the kitchen. To Captain Vinden's description of two Italian attributes, recently enunciated by him on the *Ettrick*, another could definitely be added — a love of good food. Among the prisoners were some of London's finest

ILE SAINTE HÉLÈNE

chefs and since the kitchen provisions were of first-class quality, we were eventually able to experience meals the equal of which would have been difficult to find in any of the best restaurants of Montreal.

We settled down to make the best of our circumstances. As a permanent dwelling place Camp S left a lot to be desired. Sleeping quarters were cramped and lavatory accommodation was inadequate, which led to long queues in the morning. Recreational facilities were non-existent, and the compound was far too small to accommodate 400 men at any one time.

On the plus side the food was good, and the military presence was at a minimum, although we could always see the two machine-gun towers overlooking us as we walked about in the compound. Our view across the river was spectacular, with the bridge and the magnificent vista of the city. The benefit of the view was two-edged, however, for as time passed, and with no end to our captivity in sight, the presence of the city such a short distance away served only to increase our longing for freedom. But such emotions had not as yet had time to formulate. Very few in the camp believed that our imprisonment would last for any great length of time, and so at the beginning all our energies were directed to adjusting to our new circumstances.

Camp routine was soon established. Reveille was at 7am, when the blowing of a bugle heralded the arrival of a platoon of soldiers, who stood rigidly to attention as the Union Jack was run up a flagpole in the centre of the yard. Under threat of being shot at, no prisoner was allowed into the compound before that time, but by then many of the men would be up and about inside the building, going down through the refectory into the toilet area, hoping to attend to their needs before the main body of the camp awoke. Breakfast was at 8am when we lined up at the kitchen for morning coffee and bread. Then the work parties, whose composition had already been posted up in two languages on the notice board, would begin the job of cleaning up the refectory and preparing the camp for morning roll-call and inspection.

A camp office had been set up from which the daily orders were issued, and because of my fluency in both languages and the contacts I had already established in the various factions in the camp, I was offered a job there by Moramarco. I seemed to have a natural aptitude for languages, was well on my way to understanding the various dialects of the sailors, and I found the work there very satisfying.

The cleaning and disinfecting of the latrines was a most unpleasant task, and the one to be avoided most if at all possible. After a morning's use by 400 men, the 15 loos would be well-choked and the cleaning of them was a Herculean task. This work was apportioned daily on a rota basis to each group, and the only ones excused from it were the priests, the ships officers, the Camp Leader and his office workers, the 20 or so elderly of the camp and anyone with a doctor's line for exemption. A small room at the side of the dormitories had been designated as a sick room, with Dr Rybekil, a Jewish refugee, in charge, who was kept extremely busy with applications for daily work exemptions.

By 11am the dormitories, kitchen, refectory and toilets would be clean and in order. Roll call would then take place in the compound, where we stood scruffily to attention as we were inspected by the major and counted by a sergeant. A deferential Moramarco would follow at the major's heels taking note of his many complaints, for the civilians were an untidy lot who did not conform to the standards of neatness expected by the Camp Commandant. With the roll-call over, work would start in the kitchen for the lunchtime meal which was served around 1pm.

After these activities the boredom of the day continued. The prisoners congregated in little clannish groups, sauntering idly around the compound. Groups of opposing views would be studiously avoided, and conversation would endlessly be centred around the progress of the war and the possible duration of their captivity. With the long hot afternoon over, there came a summons to the evening meal, another roll-call in the compound, then lights out and bed.

10

Mutiny

For 400 mainly fit and healthy men our daily routine was tedious, to say the least, so we greeted the military's plans for work and recreation with enthusiasm. August was drawing to a close, and with the prospect of winter not so very far away, plans had to be made for winter quarters for the soldiers who were quartered under canvas near the camp. An offer was made to the prisoners: in return for our work to build permanent soldiers' quarters we could build ourselves a recreation hut in the compound, with facilities which would include a weekly visit from a mobile cinema.

We were ecstatic, but our elation was soon dampened by the hostile reception from one section of the camp. Our cooperation would mean collaboration with the enemy, they said, and Malusa, the Fascist radio officer, made it known that anyone participating in the work would be taken note of, reported to the Fascist authorities after the war and appropriately punished.

Great argument raged in the camp, until a copy of the Geneva Convention on the treatment of PoWs was produced, and a quote from Article 50 of that document was posted on the notice-board. This article states that, among other work, duly detailed. . . *All labour connected with camp administration, installation or maintenance and not having a military purpose is permitted.*

This was pronounced upon by Captain Bonorino, who could hardly be accused of anti Italian sentiments. To the great satisfaction of most of the camp, he gave the opinion that it was perfectly proper and indeed beneficial to the prisoners for such work to be undertaken. So, despite the continuing opposition of the extreme right-wing element, who continued with their threats of retribution to anyone participating, the work parties were formed. With great enthusiasm and some expertise, for there were some joiners and carpenters among the men, the soldiers huts were soon finished.

By the middle of October work started quickly on the recreation hut, for in addition to the weekly cinema show, was the promise of a canteen where we could spend our 20 cents a day work pay. But November soon arrived and with it the beginning of the fierce cold of a Canadian winter, with temperatures falling overnight to well below zero. Ice began to form at the edge of the fast-flowing St Lawrence, heralding the complete closure of the river, which would be ice-bound in a matter of a few weeks. The camp was completely unprepared for the sudden cold. No winter clothes had as yet been distributed, and we were still clad in the lightweight uniforms issued to us on the night of our arrival. Small, pot-bellied, wood-burning stoves were hurriedly installed in the middle of the dormitories and eating areas, and we huddled round them all day long for warmth.

During the summer months, hygiene had been a simple matter. Cold showers could be taken at will, and laundry would dry out quickly in the warm atmosphere. But now even the basic rules of hygiene were difficult to carry out. Shaving in the bitterly cold toilet area had become a Spartan undertaking, and most of the men made do with clipping their whiskers with a pair of scissors. Washing oneself was difficult too and a change of clothing out of the question, for clothes could not be washed and dried. Moreover, to add to our discomfort, and despite the intense cold, the two daily roll-calls were still carried out in the open. Each morning and evening 400 cold and shivering men were rousted out of the fortress and made to stand and be counted in the frozen windswept compound.

The fact that our captors were warmly clad in heavy overcoats, their heads covered with fur hats and earmuffs, served to increase our anger. Complaints were lodged with the Camp Commandant, but he insisted that roll-call should be carried out in the open air. Proper clothing would soon be available to the prisoners, he said. Then he went on.

'The dormitories must be ventilated at least once or twice each day. You are keeping all the windows in the fortress tightly shut, thus resulting in an unhealthy atmosphere. Some fresh air can only be beneficial'.

He was probably right, for we had become a dirty unwashed bunch. We had to realise that we were prisoners, he continued, and Camp S was not a holiday camp but a prison camp. Orders had to be obeyed... or else. That stirred up memories of the first night on the island, so a sullen obedience was observed. Heavy winter clothing was issued after a few more days, but the roll-calls in the open continued, despite the ever colder weather, with the temperature falling as low as minus 25 degrees. Rumour had it that one night a soldier guard had frozen to death on the bridge above, after the heater in his sentry box had failed. Sullenness and resentment festered and grew.

One day matters came to a head. Colonel O'Donohoe (now promoted from major) carried out a spot inspection of the dormitories, did not like what he saw, and an eruption ensued.

'You are filthy and unshaven', he roared, 'and the dormitories little better than pig sties. Proper use must be made of the washing facilities and there is absolutely no excuse for your filthy state. Razors have been issued to everyone so there is no excuse for not using them. From now on everyone will have to be clean-shaven at roll-call. The dormitories will have to be vacated for a period each day and those men not occupied on the work parties will spend their time in the general areas of the building and not lying all day in their bunks as you are doing now'.

He turned to his sergeant and ordered him to see to it that these instructions were carried out. The soldier in attendance, Sergeant Le Seour, was only too well-known to the prisoners. He was a hard man. About 40 years of age, he had been reared in the lumber camps of Quebec and before rising to the rank of sergeant in the army had worked for a time as a warder in one of the tough US penitentiaries. The powers of invective and abuse he had learned were put to good use in his maintenance of discipline in the camp and amongst his own soldiers, who feared and disliked him no less than the prisoners. We remembered the weight of his hand from the night of our arrival for there were few who had not felt it on that occasion.

Since then an easy enough working relationship had developed between prisoners and guards. The group now in charge of the camp belonged to a French-Canadian Home Guard regiment, and

ISLE OF THE DISPLACED

the soldiers were all of mature years. As no great love was lost between the Quebecois and the English-Canadians, the guards were in the main sympathetic towards the Italians in the camp. But Le Seour was sympathetic to no one, and his method of sorting out the prisoners and his own men was direct and simple. In the winter, to spite us, he would keep us waiting for ten minutes at roll-call at minus 20 degrees as he ranted.

'No moving or talking in the ranks or else you get four hours on the snow party. Don't look at me that way, you fucking wop, or you'll shovel shit in the soldiers' latrines! Lousy wop bastards, lousy Jew bastards. . .'

His own soldiers fared no better and as a result the sergeant was not well regarded. For fear of possible reprisals nobody dared complain about him, not even to the genial little Captain Pitblado. In the interests of an easy life we shied clear of the ill-tempered sergeant. With his instructions completed, the Colonel departed, leaving a glowering Le Seour to confront the men. He was short and to the point.

'Tomorrow I want every one of you bastards shaved, or I'll want to know the reason why not.'

Early next morning the dormitories were a hive of activity. Every available metal mug and container had been pressed into use for the heating of water over the glowing stoves, then rushed to the toilet areas in our attempts to shave. In the absence of mirrors this was often a reciprocal affair, with many a cry of anguish as faces and necks were nicked by clumsy hands. Then came roll-call time and the 20 groups stood clean-shaven in the snow-covered compound, with faces red and smarting from our unaccustomed exposure to the freezing air. Then with the blast of a whistle to stand to attention, in marched Le Seour, face grim and ready for action. Faces were closely examined, with a searching hand occasionally testing for stubble.

Half-way down the line Le Seour stopped in front of Arturo Vivante. The case of the internment of Vivante was gone into in detail in a Penguin publication written at the war's end by A Lafitte, a Cambridge historian, with an introduction by the late Richard Crossman MP. The son of an Italian Nobel Prize winner, Arturo had been sent to boarding school in England in the late 1930s by his father to escape the anti-Semitic atmosphere then brewing up in

Italy. At the time of his arrest Arturo was just 15 years old, a small dark olive-skinned boy with dark hair and cheeks which had never felt the touch of a razor.

Le Seour looked at him closely, noticed the fine dark down on the boy's cheeks and bellowed.

'Did you shave this morning?'

'No sir,' came the trembling answer. 'I have never shaved'.

'Are you trying to make a monkey out of me?' roared the sergeant. 'I gave orders that everybody had to shave!'

And grabbing Arturo violently by the lapels of his jacket, he shook him like a rag doll and threw him backwards into a snowdrift by the side of the compound path. More frightened than hurt, Arturo rose to his feet. He was covered in snow and sobbing, with huge tears rolling down his cheeks, forming beads of ice in the intense cold.

A hum of anger arose from the assembled prisoners, which grew in volume until it seemed as if a million bees had been let loose. A snowball flew through the air, hitting Le Seour squarely on top of the head, to be followed by a barrage aimed in his general direction. Not all the snowballs were well-directed, many landed harmlessly on the ground, but a good proportion of them struck home, covering him from head to foot in a mantle of snow.

With a yell Le Seour drew his truncheon, bent on revenge, but the accompanying officer, realising quickly that the situation was about to turn ugly, blew several sharp blasts on his whistle. In the flash of an eye the compound filled with soldiers and the prisoners were herded back into their quarters, leaving a snow-covered sergeant spluttering in anger.

Back in the fortress, the implication of what had happened began to sink in. Some groups of timorous prisoners regretted the spontaneous reaction to the attack on young Arturo, which, after all, had been more spectacular than dangerous. Memories of that first night came flooding back, and there was much hand-wringing and fearful speculation. I had been as resentful as anyone during the past few weeks, and had been as vociferous as anyone in my complaints about the lack of clothing.

Anger welled up inside me at the treatment meted out to little Arturo, so I conferred for a moment with some of my group, jumped on to a table the better to be seen, and shouted for attention in Italian.

ISLE OF THE DISPLACED

'What are you afraid of,' I shouted. 'They're not going to kill us for throwing snowballs at a sergeant! If they had wanted to do that they could easily have done it the first night. What can they do to us? Put us in jail? We're there already. Are we men or what?' And sensing their attention increasing, I went on.

'We have started something, so let's see it through. Let's stick together for our rights. Let's call a strike, no cooperation with the military, no work parties, no services of any kind to the soldiers, no roll-call. Nobody goes into the compound for any reason whatsoever. This is the time to demand our rights under the Geneva Convention!'

I waved a much-thumbed copy of the document aloft.

'We have the right to a visit from an International Red Cross representative. Now's the time to get decent conditions. There are enough rations in the kitchen to last for several days if properly used, and enough fuel for a short time too.'

Carried away with my own rhetoric, and with the calculated intention of eliciting support, I turned to the Fascist group.

'What does your Duce say? *Meglio vivere un giorno da leone che cent' anni da pecora.*'[1]

Rather pleased with my own histrionics, I jumped down and let others take up the theme. Finally shouts of approval drowned out the few faint voices of dissent. A quick plan of procedure was drawn up by the group leaders, who to a man favoured such a course of action, and so began the great mutiny of Camp S.

---

[1] 'Better to live one day as a lion, than a hundred years as a sheep.'

11
Negotiation

At one end of the fort a long, broad passage connecting the main block to some outhouses had been partitioned into two: on one side was the prisoners' office and on the other was the commandant's quarters and working area for his staff. An intercom connected the two offices and within an hour of the incidents in the compound a bell rang in the colonel's office. Permission to come through was granted and a delegation of four prisoners, including me, was escorted into the officer's presence. Standing respectfully to attention, Moramarco began reading from a hastily typewritten sheet.

Firstly, he stated that it was hoped that no one had been hurt by the snowball incident in the courtyard: it was also hoped that the provocation behind the affair was understood by the colonel.

Secondly, until certain reasonable requests had been granted, a state of mutiny would exist in the camp. The men had decided that until then no one would leave the buildings for any reason whatsoever. No work parties would function, no roll-call would be attended, all services to the officers and men would cease. The requests were as follows:

1. Roll-call to be held indoors during the winter months.

2. It was known that there were toilet areas with a hot-water supply within the fortress which were at present off-limits to the men. These should be made available to all prisoners.

3. Since the present sick room was utterly inadequate, proper medical facilities should be provided.

4. Lack of news was destructive to morale, therefore a newspaper should be allowed into the camp.

5. No general punishment should be imposed for the events of that day.

6. As laid out in the Geneva Convention, a Red Cross representative should be asked to visit the camp.

The note was handed to an impassive colonel, and we withdrew to rejoin our expectant comrades. If they had expected a quick response to our requests, they were doomed to disappointment. Four days passed without the slightest indication that the authorities were in the least concerned about the strike. Through the narrow windows we could see that the guards outside the barbed wire had been doubled, and that an extra man stood beside the machine guns in the towers. Any attempt to lean out of any window would be greeted by several rifle shots fired into the air, but apart from that it was as if we had been forgotten by the outside world.

Four days is a long time for 400 men to be cooped up together in a small space with nothing to do except wait for an axe to fall, and voices of complaint and dissent soon made themselves heard. With a few exceptions, opinion as to the wisdom of the strike predictably followed political leanings. The Jews were mainly against, and condemned the action as stupid and pointless. They claimed that constant representation to the authorities would have brought about the desired result, but ignored the fact that for weeks now the camp leadership had been asking for the things that we were now striking for.

The exception was the lawyer Tagiuri, who on the *Ettrick* had spoken up about the transportation of internees across a war zone. The military were definitely in breach of the Geneva Convention, he claimed, and the camp was fully justified in taking the present course of action even if it meant having to face great discomfort. Predictably the Fascists were 100 per cent in favour, but for different reasons. We should never have cooperated with the authorities in the first place, they said, and everything possible should be done to embarrass the enemy. It was everybody's duty as good Italians to resist the enemy and in so doing they would be doing their duty by *Il Duce*, they argued.

The ringleaders found unexpected support from the little Spanish war veteran, Aldo Gatti. The conditions we were being made to live in were deplorable, he said. Here we were in Canada with millions and millions of acres of empty land and here we were herded together like chickens. Such oppression and injustice had to be fought wherever it was found.

NEGOTIATION

As for myself, almost from the beginning I had begun to regret the bravado that had spurred me on to advocate such a course of action, for now I honestly could not see that any good would come of it. We had no cards to play. We were completely at the mercy of our captors, I thought, and my brave face and words of cheer to my comrades did not reflect the reality of my inner feelings.

Discontent began to make itself evident with every passing hour. Lack of exercise and confinement made everyone irritable, and squabbles and fist fights broke out at the slightest provocation. Food was severely rationed and accusations of corruption and favouritism in the management of the provisions were beginning to make themselves heard. Stocks of wood for heating would not last much longer, and with 20 degrees of frost outside we could well freeze to death if a settlement was not reached. The idea of surrender began to spread among the men.

The middle of the road civilians, caught up in the original euphoria of the strike, began to voice their doubts. What were they hoping to achieve with all this?, they asked. Life wasn't really so bad before, they said. Nobody had bothered them much since that first night. So why rock the boat? The food was good. So what if there was no hot water. . . so you had to stand in the cold for a few minutes at roll-call. . . so all the news you got was second-hand and maybe not true. . . so what? The war would take its course whether they knew anything about it or not, so what were they striking for? What would they do if the soldiers started kicking us around as they had done the first night? They had been stupid to listen to that show-off Joe with all his big talk. No one thought to mention the Arturo Vivante incident that had sparked it all off, and so the mutiny began slowly to crumble.

Then one morning the old sailor Godizzaro was found dead in his bunk. An old man of indeterminate age, the old sailor had been unwell for some time, and had lain passively in his bunk since the beginning of the strike. He had refused the food brought to him by his companions and had died in the night, as quietly and as unobtrusively as he had lived. The intercom, unused for the last four days, gave the news to the authorities, who responded by sending in a stretcher on which the body was laid, covered by a blanket and taken across the ice-encrusted compound to the gates by a sad little cortege of his comrades. The news of Godizzaro's death deepened the gloom in the camp, if that were possible, but it was as though the old man's death had set some wheels in motion, for some moments later the prisoners' representative was summoned to the colonel's office.

The petition had been examined, he said, and whilst the prisoners could well be left to stew in their own juice, in the interests of humanity the following decisions had been reached:

1. Henceforth during excessively cold weather roll-call would be held under cover, the suitability of the weather to be agreed upon by both sides each day.

2. Additional latrines and wash areas would be made available.

3. Newspapers would not circulate in the camp, but a newspaper would be posted up each day for reading.

4. The camp in general would not be punished for the snowball incident, but the affair could not be overlooked, so the person who had thrown the first one would have to give himself up for suitable punishment.

5. A Red Cross representative would be asked to visit the camp.

The prisoners had to make a pretence of consultation before agreeing to the terms, but of course, given the state of camp morale the men were on the point of surrender anyhow, and any terms would have been acceptable to them.

They were delighted with the outcome, each faction finding in it a justification for their own point of view, the activists claiming that without the strike nothing would have been achieved, whilst the opponents of the action claimed that the concessions would have come about anyway.

Everyone had forgotten about Le Seour, whose action at roll-call had sparked the whole thing off. It was rumoured on the grapevine that he had been hauled over the coals by the colonel for his assault on young Vivante. His visits to the camp became subdued and few and far between, and he eventually disappeared completely, presumably having been transferred elsewhere.

However, not only the cynics took note of the fact that exactly five days after the end of the mutiny, Camp S had its first visit from an International Red Cross representative. Because of the time factor the visit obviously could not have been as the result of our demands. It must have been long in the pipeline, and it would have been rather embarrassing for the authorities had it taken place in the middle of a full-blown mutiny.

There remained the finding of a scapegoat. To the accompaniment of cheers, one Ciritiello, nicknamed *'u scemo'* (the idiot) by his Sicilian shipmates, proudly marched to his incarceration in one of the three punishment cells, which was the first time any of them had been used.

After 30 days he emerged to be greeted by his cheering comrades and a fatherly pat on the head from Captain Bonorino, thus putting the seal on his brief moment of glory, earned by confessing to a crime he had never committed.

12
Tension

Moramarco had been an abject failure as Camp Leader. His was a vain and self-centred personality, obsessed with the maintenance of his personal appearance with no thought whatsoever for the well-being of the prisoners. His sole concern was *fare bella figura*, to cut a good figure in front of his fellow prisoners and their captors. His vanity was such that somehow he had managed to squeeze all sorts of personal concessions from the pliable O'Donohoe. One of these was permission for his personal use of a separate toilet facility at the far end of the compound to separate him from the common herd. His behaviour at the time of the mutiny was ineffectual, diametrically opposed to the leadership that the prisoners had a right to expect on such a critical occasion. His poverty of character can perhaps be illustrated by the following incident which took place prior to the mutiny:

After several months in the camp the first letters and parcels began to arrive for the civilian internees from their families in the UK, whose fears that their loved ones might have shared the fate of the dead on the *Arandora Star* had finally been put at rest. I was one of the first to receive a parcel and in it my parents had included, amongst other items, articles of supreme luxury — three bars of Palmolive toilet soap. The carbolic slabs of so-called soap issued to the prisoners served only to irritate even the thickest of skins, and the possession of toilet soap made me a man much envied by my fellow prisoners. Remembering the kindness done to me by Dino Orsi at Woodhouselea, I presented him with one bar of the soap, and was then incessantly pestered by Moramarco for a share in the remaining two. His skin was being ruined by the rough camp soap, complained Moramarco, his good looks were being put at risk. I didn't really need the toilet soap. Mine was a tough peasant skin and he would do me any favour for one of the bars. As one rather blunt sailor put it, *'Per un pezzo di quel sapone quello ti darebbe anche il culo.'*[1]

So I struck a bargain, for a bar of soap Moramarco had to give me access to the officers' mess where I could see how free people ate and lived. We had in the camp some fine musicians who had formed a quartet with the use of musical instruments supplied by an organisation known as the War Prisoners Aid of the YMCA and the group sometimes played in the mess to entertain the officers' guests. So, despite the fact that I didn't know a single note of music, Moramarco arranged for me to sit for one night in the mess with the musicians. I sat there like an idiot and held a mandolin very professionally, got fed up after ten minutes and wished I had never given up my precious soap for the sake of watching a bunch of rather plain females eat some food. Perhaps this silly incident said something about my character too!

However, immediately after the mutiny the despised Moramarco was replaced by the young Martinez, whose cultured yet firm demeanour created a good impression both on the military and on the prisoners whom he represented. One of his first acts was to cancel all the privileges which Moramarco had gained for himself — a very popular act.

The camp had no sooner been tidied up after the mutiny and work on the recreation hut restarted, when the visit of the Red Cross Representative was announced. The camp was subjected to an inspection by a group made up of the colonel and one other officer. George Martinez accompanied the Red Cross official on his tour of inspection.

Under his discreet and subtle guidance the inspection party was steered to controversial parts of the camp. The inspection was a thorough one, with many questions asked and notes taken. An unsupervised interview of randomly chosen prisoners was asked for and three questions were put to some of them.

How was the food? How were they being treated? Was there any comment the prisoner cared to make?

All agreed on the excellence of the food, most mentioned the punishment meted out on the first night, but added that there were

---

[1] 'He'd give you his arse for a piece of that soap.'

no complaints now. Most complaints related to the lack of space, absence of recreational facilities and lack of any work to relieve the boredom of daily life.

The Red Cross visitor listened sympathetically to our comments, shook hands all round, and left us with the hope that some good would accrue to the camp from the visit. This was in fact the case, for in a very short time Red Cross parcels began to arrive, but since these, amongst other things, contained items of food, it was evident that no special thought had been given to the requirements of individual camps. However, two very welcome gifts were received by the camp as a result of the visit. One was a crate of assorted books in Italian and English donated by the YMCA and the other, a wireless set.

This wireless created a buzz of excitement in the camp. Finally we could get news from the outside world! After the strike, work had been very quickly finished on the prisoners' recreation hut, which meant that there was a place other than the refectory or dormitories where a man could pass some time during daylight hours. Pride of place was given here to the radio. A little canteen had been rigged up in one corner as well and here cigarettes and chocolates could be bought by those fortunate enough to have been earning the 20 cents per day work party money. The YMCA also donated a ping-pong table and a chess set was available for those so minded. But the focal point was the radio set. This offered a whole new dimension to the prisoners. Some literally sat from morning until night with ears glued to the loudspeaker, anxious for any piece of war news that might have any bearing on their incarceration.

For Italy the news was anything but good. In October of 1940 Mussolini had invaded Greece and Yugoslavia and now in late December news was coming through of Italian reversals there. In November the Italian army had suffered a crushing defeat at Croaitza in Greece, and German panzer groups had been sent to avoid a complete collapse on that front. In the same month seven Italian warships had been sunk off the coast of Sardinia, while from North Africa there was news of the disastrous reverses in the desert, with the Italians surrendering in droves to the British forces.

There was news also of the sacking of Marshal Badoglio, Commander-in-Chief of the Italian army. Italo Balbo, the air force hero who had achieved international fame in 1933 when he

TENSION

commanded a squadron of 24 flying boats on a flight from Italy to the World Fair in Chicago, (an incredible feat at the time), was reported dead in Libya, shot down by his own men, it was said. The news commentators made much also of the arrival of the first contingent of the Afrika Korps in North Africa; the Italian defeats in Greece were being repeated on a much larger scale in Libya and Egypt and there too the Germans had to come to the help of their incompetent allies, crowed the newsreaders.

A running translation of all these bad tidings was given on the spot to those who did not speak English, usually by myself or by one of the other bilingual prisoners who happened to be there at the time. These long and seemingly interminable lists of Italian reverses were greeted with cries of rage and patriotic fury by the merchant seamen and their officers, who, together with other self-styled Fascist patriots, dismissed it all as false British propaganda. Malusa, keeper of the little black book, let it be known that he was taking note and that anyone spreading such patently false enemy news would be dealt with after the certain Italian victory.

The news bulletins told too of the constant heavy air raids on Britain. London was being bombed nightly and the raids had reached as far north as Glasgow, where the Clydebank shipbuilding area had been very heavily bombed. Some of the prisoners came from these areas, and with families still living there, fear for their loved ones was added to the stress of their daily lives.

Displeased with the bad news from the radio, someone, obviously from the ranks of the Fascists, resorted to a simple course of action. The Nazi principle of book burning was applied: if it says something contrary to your beliefs, burn it. One morning the radio was found smashed to pieces.

This brought to the surface the simmering tensions in the camp, which were kept in check by the ubiquitous presence of the soldiers, for the camp had been warned of the dire consequences should violence ever break out in the compound. The many political affiliations and the latent danger they posed to the minority groups were by this time well known to the authorities. Many requests had been made to them by the Jews and the left-wing groups that they should be separated from the rest of the prisoners, because they were, after all, natural enemies, and should never have been sharing common quarters.

These requests had also been made to the Red Cross representative, who had listened sympathetically to the minority delegations. He had pointed out that the mixing of all these disparate groups had been the action of the British Government and that it was up to that government to rectify any mistakes it might have made in the matter. His remit was to establish that decent conditions prevailed in the prison camps, and not to pass judgement on the act of internment itself.

The colonel in charge had long since been made aware of the potentially explosive situation inside his camp, for by now outside forces had been at work questioning the arrest of many of those behind the wire, and behind the scenes there had been much political activity with the aim of obtaining the quick release of the Jews in the camp. But until these decisions were made, the camp had to remain constituted as it was; a mixture of conflicting political views that were always on the brink of exploding into open conflict. So the colonel had made it plain that any violence inside the compound would be followed by the strongest possible reaction by him, a threat which had until now maintained an uneasy peace amongst the men.

The loss of the radio was bad enough but restraint was thrown to the wind when the newspaper posted daily on the notice-board was vandalised by some of the sailors. Harsh words were exchanged. Accusations of anti-Italian feeling were replied to with counter-accusations that Mussolini and the *Fascisti* were nothing more than trained monkeys on Hitler's leash. More to the point, the anti-Fascists said the Fascist destruction of news sources was motivated by fear that what they heard was the truth, and that the war was not going as they wanted. Scuffles and fights broke out at the slightest provocation. On one occasion Gatti, the little Spanish war veteran, had to be stopped from half-killing Malusa, whom he blamed, rightly or wrongly, for the destruction of the radio. The situation in the camp was now so ugly that the colonel. had to resort to the presence of one or two groups of uniformed military police inside the wire in order to ensure that no violence erupted among us.

Despite all this however, in common with some other prisoners whose jobs brought them into daily contact with all members of the camp, I circulated freely amongst the warring groups. I enjoyed the stimulus of conversation with so many different people of so many divergent views. I took special pleasure in my contact with the merchant seamen. My natural ear for languages enabled me to follow their conversation, heavily accented though it was with native dialect, and the friendly open manner which I assumed with them helped to break down the suspicion with which they viewed the *Inglesi* in general.

I soon realised that the seamen's criticism of other groups in the camp stemmed from fear and ignorance: fear that they would incur the displeasure of their officers and then be punished if they did not follow all directives obediently; fear for themselves and their families if they should be in some way be disadvantaged by their superiors and fear of *olio e manganello* (oil and truncheon).[1] Their ignorance stemmed from their illiteracy, derived from the poorer and more backward parts of southern Italy, which made them completely dependant on their superiors for all information about the outside world. Their illiteracy gave them a feeling of inferiority before their officers, whom they regarded as somehow superior in the order of things and to be listened to and obeyed in all matters. Ignorance also explained their unquestioning acceptance of the slogans of Fascism, for every man, no matter how humble, has the need within him to feel a little greatness in his soul, and from this need stemmed the blind acceptance of the constantly repeated slogans of *Il Duce,* which spoke of the greatness of the new Italy of which they formed a part.

For most of them, contact with the English and Scots-Italians was their first long-term experience of people used to freedom of thought and expression and so the intelligent ones among them began to seek out the company of the bilingual elements in the camp and profit from their new contacts.

---

[1] The Fascist punishment in Italy was a good beating and a dose of half-a-litre of castor oil, which was forced down the throat.

13
Mr Paterson

The fact that in the middle of the dangers confronting Britain in 1940 the government was able to find the time and the will to examine both the moral question raised by the sudden internment of thousands of people without trial and also the possible miscarriage of justice in the process was remarkable. At the time of the sweeping round-up of enemy aliens and persons arrested under Regulation 18b of the Emergency Powers Bill of 1939, which permitted the arrest of any person, irrespective of nationality, who might be a security risk in time of war, voices criticised the draconian measures taken at the fall of France and Italy's declaration of war on Britain. For this war, unlike any other conflict which had gone before, was not only a war of nation against nation, but also a war of conflicting ideologies. On one side were the Fascist dictatorships with their emphasis on the all-embracing power of the state, without regard to the personal liberty or philosophy of the individual. On the other were the liberal democracies with their concepts of tolerance, human rights and freedom of the individual.

There were many anti-Fascist Italians and anti-Nazi Germans either living permanently in Britain or sheltering as refugees there after the purges and racial persecution carried out by their respective regimes. Many came from Germany, where tens of thousands of Jews and political dissidents had been forced to flee the threat of the Nazi concentration camps. The mass arrest of these categories in the summer of 1940, although perfectly justifiable on the grounds of expediency, occasioned many a doubt in the minds of some liberally minded British public figures. Prominent among these was the Labour MP George Strauss who raised questions in Parliament about the arrest of German and Austrian Jewish refugees who were known anti-Nazis. Before the outbreak of war with Germany a Parliamentary committee on refugees had been set up under the chairmanship of Miss Eleanor Rathbone MP, and she too became concerned about the arrests of many of the persons who had come to Britain to escape Nazi persecution.

When the internment of Italians began the arrests seemed to be even more indiscriminate, and on July 9 the Manchester *Guardian* began a series of articles on the matter. Cases were cited of the arrests of persons who had sons and brothers in the British army. Prominence was given in one report dated July 17 to the case of a British soldier, evacuated from Dunkirk, who came home on leave to find his father behind barbed wire.[1] On August 6, Lord Cecil, the High Commissioner for refugees made a powerful speech in the House of Lords highlighting these matters and criticised the Home Office in the strongest possible terms for its policy on the internment of aliens. He cited the case of one of the victims of the sinking of the *Arandora Star*. Silvestro D'Ambrogio of Hamilton was 68 years old and had been living in Britain for 42 years. He had two sons serving in the British army and another son in the Canadian Expeditionary Force. On August 22 time was given in the House of Commons for a short debate on this matter and during it Sir John Anderson, the Home Secretary made the following admission:

'I am not here to deny that most regrettable and deplorable things have happened in connection with the internment camps. I regret them deeply. They have been due partly to the inevitable haste with which the policy of internment had to be carried out. They were due, however, in some cases, to mistakes of individuals, stupidity, muddling. These things all relate to the past. So far as we can remedy mistakes we shall remedy them.'

In view of all this, a commission was set up to examine the whole question. The members of this commission included Clement Atlee and Herbert Morrison, the latter soon to become Home Secretary in the war-time coalition government. The deportation of civilian internees to Australia and Canada raised some disturbing and awkward questions. Nothing could be done about the 721 dead of the *Arandora Star*, but a Home Office representative was

---

[1] The soldier was Sergeant Santangeli of the Highland Light Infantry and this incident is described in chapter 4.

despatched to Canada with power to examine individual cases and make recommendations. It may be perhaps of interest to note that all the initiatives in the righting of any wrongs done to individual internees were taken by left-wing politicians. In late November 1940, this official, Alexander Paterson, arrived in Montreal, and with specific reference to the camp on Ile Sainte Hélène, which was the only Italian camp in Canada, set up an office there and made himself available to any prisoner who might want to complain about the justice of his internment.

His arrival was rapturously greeted by the majority of the civilians. The Jewish group were unreservedly elated at the prospect of being freed from the tensions of the camp. They were to a man genuine refugees from Fascism, and to have found themselves imprisoned side by side with people representative of their persecutors was stressful to say the least. A large number of the rest of the civilians also had cause for resentment and complaint about their arrests and they too welcomed the opportunity of having their cases heard and their wrongs righted. About 100 names were submitted for interview with Paterson. The camp buzzed with a mixture of hope, expectation, and criticism. The Fascist section of the camp labelled anyone going to speak with the Home Office representative as an anti-Fascist, and Malusa's little black book was kept busy with the names of anyone seen entering the section of the camp where Mr Paterson's office was situated. Without a doubt many were deterred from even talking to the man, for the general opinion in the camp was still of an Axis victory, and the fear of postwar reprisals was strong.

Alexander Paterson was startled by what he found in the camp, and a copy of his report to the Home Office can be inspected there and in the public record section of the Dominion's Office. He was amazed to find that such a high proportion of the civilians spoke no Italian, and found it difficult to believe that the broad Scots and Cockney accents of many of the persons who came into his office were spoken from the lips of Italian nationals.

To most of them he could make only limited promises, however. In no case could he guarantee a release if he found the person worthy of return to the UK but only internment on the Isle of Man pending a review of each case. He could, however, give the assurance that under Clause 22 of the new regulations governing internment which stated that favourable consideration would be given to any one who had lived in Great Britain since childhood, release was very probable. Many of the internees were faced with a dilemma. The memory of their sufferings on the *Ettrick* was only too fresh in their minds. With the knowledge which they now had about the sinking of the *Arandora Star* and the death of hundreds of their Warth Mills colleagues, was the dangerous journey across the Atlantic worth the risk simply for the possible exchange of one internment camp for another? Argument for and against raged among the civilians, and at the end of it all only a comparative handful, together with most of the Jewish refugees and Communists asked Paterson that they be returned to Britain.

The majority of those interviewed by Paterson who, always patient, made himself available for almost two months to anyone who cared to see him, elected to remain where they were to pursue independent applications for release. Mr Paterson returned to Britain in July 1941 having visited German internment camps in Canada with the same objective in mind. His visit reflected credit on a nation during a critical moment in its fight for survival.

Many private representations were made on behalf of individual prisoners, the one notable example being that of the young Arturo Vivante, the Jewish refugee at the centre of the Sergeant Le Soeur incident. Ruth Draper, the well-known American actress, had been a close friend of the Vivante family since a long sojourn of hers in Italy in the early 1930s. In 1940, hearing of the boy's internment in Canada, Miss Draper started a vigorous campaign for his release. On Arturo's behalf she personally approached the Canadian Prime Minister McKenzie King. Such was the strength of her argument and the justice of her cause that in the summer of 1941 Vivante was set free in Canada where he lived for a while. In 1950 the *New Yorker* magazine published a short story by him, The Stream, in which he mentions his stay in the Montreal internment camp. He tells of his arrest whilst in a boarding school in North Wales, his separation from his father and brother who were sent to the Isle of Man, and of their fear that he had been lost in the sinking of the *Arandora Star*. He tells also of the efforts of a close family friend to have him freed, of how difficult it was to adjust to freedom after a year of confinement, and of how the sight of a policeman in uniform would awaken in him the fear of once again being arrested and put behind the barbed-wire fence.

In the late summer of 1941, as a result of Paterson's visit, about 45 internees were returned to Britain. The Jewish group departed en masse, accompanied by a handful of others who felt with good reason that they could no longer put up with the stresses and tensions of Camp S. They preferred to face the dangers of an Atlantic crossing in the expectation of possible release once back in the UK.

I was sorry to see many of them go, for they were, especially the Jews, the intellectual cream of the prisoners and I had enjoyed the stimulus of contact with them. However the departure of this group had a marked effect on the tensions which had kept the camp in a state of constant turmoil. Many of the persons who opted to return to Britain had been often abrasively and openly pro-British in their attitudes, in a situation where discretion would have been more advisable. Their departure, although much regretted on the one hand, made for a much more relaxed atmosphere in the camp.

Another who left was Sam Corti. His genial personality and bubbling good humour had made him popular amongst all sections of the camp.

Sam was born in Glasgow about 30 years before, of two immigrant Italians, and had grown up bilingual, completely at home in both languages. As was the almost general custom in immigrant Italian families then, as soon as Sam reached the age of 14 he was taken from school and put to work in the family business, in his case a busy East-end café. An energetic, athletic type, Sam found work behind a counter intensely boring, and looked forward to his twice-yearly visits to Italy where he spent a fortnight on each visit training in a *Balilla* camp.

The *Balilla* was an organisation for boys and youths modelled on the Boy Scout movement in Britain, but with a distinct difference — it was purely militaristic in concept. The boys wore smart black uniforms with a tasselled cap, trained with imitation guns, and were subjected to a military-style discipline. All kinds of sporting activities and social events were laid on that were tinged with skilful Fascist propaganda, calculated to indoctrinate youthful minds.

The organisation was for boys of up to 15 years of age, and on passing that age Sam found that if he wanted to continue his paid visits to Italy, he would have to join the *Avanguardisti*, (the Italian equivalent of the British Territorial Army). This he did, but now the training involved real guns and real soldiers.

During one of his periods in Italy, the Civil War began in Spain. Despite all the non-intervention pacts agreed to by the major powers in the conflict, Russia sent help to the Republican side, and Germany and Italy, not to be outdone, intervened on the side of Franco. So Sam, instead of being allowed away after his two weeks training period found himself assigned, whether he liked it or not, to the famous *Littorio* infantry division. This division was under the command of the General Roatta who was later to achieve notoriety on the Yugoslav Front fighting against the Serbs in late 1940. Very soon Sam found himself on a troopship on its way to Valencia, a port under the rebels' control, in the company of young soldiers of his own age, full of high spirits and looking forward to the glamorous adventures to come.

But real war was a far sight removed from the games he had played in the *Balilla*, and Sam did not enjoy being shot at whilst tramping around in the freezing mud of a cold Spanish winter. However, he did his duty as well as the next man, and in an action on the Guadalajara front he was instrumental in saving the life of his major who had been severely wounded by shell-fire. This was a deed of some propaganda value back in Italy and soon Sam found himself back in Rome on the receiving end of a medal pinned on his chest by the great Duce himself. In the meantime his father back in Glasgow was deteriorating in health, so on compassionate grounds Sam was demobbed with honour and was soon back behind the counter of the family shop doling out ice-cream wafers. Strangely enough, yet perhaps not so strangely, for in those days news reportage of an international nature was not as comprehensive as it is today, not a whisper of Sam's exploits had ever percolated back to Glasgow. Then at the time of Italy's declaration of war on Britain, Sam, as a British subject born in Glasgow, received his call-up papers from the British army, and was ordered to report to Maryhill barracks to begin his military service.

Sam had no desire whatsoever to serve again in any army. His experience on the cold Guadalajara plateau had cured him of any inclination to play soldier, and he did not relish the possibility of fighting against the comrades he had served with not so long ago. He thought long and hard, and was still thinking as he stood in front of a little major in a room at the barracks. He waited as the officer consulted some papers.

'Now Corti, I see here that your parents were born in Italy?'

'Yes Sir', answered Sam with a little nervous cough.

'Do you speak Italian?' Conveniently forgetting that he was fluent in both languages, Sam pondered for a second. 'Just a wee bit, Sir,' clearing his throat again nervously.

'You know that Italy is now at war with us, so I'll have to get some background from you. Can you drive a car? Were you ever in the Boy Scouts? Do you have any special ability?' Sam coughed again.

'No Sir, I was never in the Scouts, but I served for a year in the *Littorio* division of the Italian army under General Roatta, and I fought in the battle of Guadalajara in Spain.' Again a nervous cough.

'. . .and I was decorated by Mussolini with the Silver Military Cross for bravery in action.'

He spread out his Italian military papers in front of the flabbergasted officer, topped them off with a photograph of a beaming *Duce* in the act of pinning a medal on his chest, and stepped back to await the major's reaction.

The officer pawed feverishly through the papers and paused to look at the photo of Sam, standing stiffly to attention in front of *Il Duce*. His face slowly began to change colour until it finally became a vivid puce. He let out a roar and then came to his senses.

'SERGEANT!' he bellowed. 'SERGEANT! Take this man and lock him up in the cells!'

Sam was intensively questioned by a battery of Intelligence Officers about his *Balilla* activities and his military service in Spain. Through it all he felt quite badly done to. What had he done wrong? Britain wasn't at war with Italy during his period in the Italian military, so what was everybody on about?

But Sam was duly interned under Regulation 18B, and in due course found himself a prisoner in the camp at Woodhouselea, then on to Warth Mills, the *Ettrick*, and eventually to Camp S in Montreal. But internment camp life did not suit him in the least, so he sought an interview with Mr Paterson, as a result of which he returned to the UK, was enlisted in the British army and finished the War as a sergeant in the Pioneer Corps, helping to clear bomb damage in the streets of London.

MR PATERSON

He was a cheery, effervescent, character well liked by all in the camp. The Fascist element could not point a finger at him, having been decorated by the great *Duce* himself, and his reasons for wanting to return to his home in Glasgow were fully understood and shared by his colleagues.

14
Work

Given the lack of official compulsion to take part in organised work, and the purely voluntary nature of the outside work parties, it would have been very easy for us to sink into a routine of slothful apathy. Many did, and performed only the most basic of tasks which consisted of eating, sleeping, and allowing themselves to be counted twice a day. But most men instinctively need activity, and so every day most of us tried to keep busy in an attempt to ignore the unpleasant reality of our camp existence. The official work parties were always oversubscribed. By the summer of 1941 various kinds of work had been made available to the prisoners. About a quarter of a mile from the camp there stood an old stone building called *la Poudrière* (the Powderhouse), presumably because at one time it served as a munitions store for the fortress. This was put into use as a joinery shop and provided work for about 30 men who made wooden packing cases and simple articles of furniture.

A small workshop for the packaging of Red Cross bandages had been erected inside the compound and this also provided work for a dozen or so prisoners. A place in the Powderhouse work party was much sought after. To work there meant leaving the confines of the barbed wire and a change of surroundings. The march to and from the building, albeit under heavily-armed guard, was a tonic. To be able to walk in a straight line for more than a few hundred feet; to be away from the milling mass of men in the compound; to see and smell the leafy perfume of shrubs and trees, was enjoyment indeed.

The establishment of these two workplaces again gave rise to bitter controversy in the camp. The Fascists labelled as traitors anyone participating in what they claimed was work calculated to help the enemy. A visit to the camp was made by Red Cross officials who quoted the by now famous Geneva Convention. They assured the prisoners that such work was permitted by the regulations, but their assurance was to no avail, and the Fascists remained firmly opposed. To their chagrin, a vote was held on the matter by the prisoners, who came down solidly in favour of the proposed work, but this decision created further tensions in the camp, for the Fascists then claimed that since no voting was allowed in Italy such a procedure had no place in an Italian camp! It was significant that a high proportion of the sailors were strongly and openly in favour of the projects, which showed that they were beginning to think for themselves in these matters.

The authorities were asked to provide yet more work, and so the island cleaning parties were formed. These consisted of groups of 20 prisoners or so, armed with an assortment of wheelbarrows, shovels, brooms and rakes. They were taken out to all parts of the island under guard to tidy up the many roads and pathways bisecting it. This work also was much sought after, since it too gave the possibility of spending time outside the wire. In the winter months so-called snow parties were formed. Brooms and rakes were exchanged for long-handled snow shovels and the men were put to clearing roads blocked by the frequent and heavy falls of snow. But work on the snow parties was not very popular, because it entailed working in sub-zero temperatures with the thermometer showing as much as 20 or 30 degrees below zero. At these temperatures a man's breath would literally freeze at his nostrils, with beads of ice forming around his nose and lips. Moreover, although the winter uniforms were of thick felt material with heavy ear-muffed caps, layers of underclothing had to be worn to protect against the intense cold. The exertion of wielding the shovels heavy with snow would make the men break sweat, which would then chill on the skin, making it almost impossible to remain warm.

Care too had to be taken to urinate before setting out in such low temperatures. Peeing in such conditions was a risky and complicated procedure. Some with a perverse sense of humour would return from the snow party carrying slivers of amber-coloured ice to throw at their comrades back in the warm dormitories of the fort, a practise not surprisingly stamped out on the grounds of hygiene.

Occasionally, after exceptionally heavy snow falls had swamped the Montreal street-cleaning facilities, volunteers would be asked for and then escorted into the city under heavy guard to help clear the streets. In the winter months these groups wearing blue uniforms with red discs and stripes became a familiar sight to the citizens of Montreal. The heavy guard was a precaution against fraternisation, for many French-Canadians were politically hostile to the English and would attempt to talk to the men, sympathising with their lot and offering gifts of chocolates and cigarettes to them. This work was never very popular, even though the participants could be sure of returning to the camp laden with goodies, because many considered it a humiliation to be paraded thus in full view of the local population.

The political hostility to the English was evidently shared by some Canadian politicians, for in the summer of 1942 the camp was graced for a short time by the presence of Mayor Houde of Montreal. He was an advocate of an independent Quebec, and had been removed from office and arrested for his persistent speeches in criticism of the English and his exhortation to French Canadians to resist conscription into the Canadian army. He was kept in the camp for about a month, then placed under house arrest for the remainder of the war. Politically, his arrest proved to be of no embarrassment whatsoever. On his release after the war he was re-elected mayor of Montreal with a thumping majority.

To a great extent our way of life in the camp depended on the whims of the commanding officer and the nature of the soldiers in direct contact with us. The ones who had been so enthusiastic and vigorous on our reception night belonged to an English-Canadian regiment and although no further violence was delivered, they rigidly enforced discipline. Orders were barked at us in best parade ground fashion, and any slowness or reluctance on our part was dealt with none-too-gentle pushes and nudges with rifle butts. A few months later they were relieved by ageing French-Canadian home guard types, who were friendly enough, and not nearly as strict as their predecessors. The guards were changed every few months or so, and we soon learned to adapt to differing degrees of discipline or the lack of it. We always cheered the arrival of French-Canadian units. With the strong anti-English secessionist movement in Quebec, the Quebecois soldiers looked upon us as more sinned

WORK

against than sinning. Life under them was relatively easy, discipline was lax, and the work parties were not made to break sweat.

The camp officers were not attached to any specific regiment, but they too seemed to be subject to a rota system. One day, about two years after the opening of the camp, Captain Pitblado reappeared on the scene. He was as rotund and as avuncular as ever, and his dialogue had not been rewritten. He must have forgotten his first posting to our camp; his walkabout and his homilies were exactly the same as they were then. 'You play ball with me lads, and I'll play ball with you.'

This was when Bosco joined the prisoners. One day an island work party returned to base followed by a large, bedraggled, emaciated and flea-ridden sheep dog. Obviously a stray, it had hung around the prisoners all day, hungrily wolfing down the scraps thrown at it during meal breaks. Next morning the dog was still at the gates. It followed the work group all day long, devoured the scraps thrown at it, and again bedded down for the night at the camp gates. Captain Pitblado was approached. Would he kindly ask the Camp Commandant for permission to take the dog in, delouse it, and keep it as a camp mascot? Permission was given, the dog was scrubbed, disinfected, and given the name Bosco. Regular and plentiful food fattened him up, and after a few weeks the camp had a large, handsome and affectionate sheep dog as a mascot. He ambled around all day, occasionally went out with the work parties, and became as much part of the camp as we were. Each morning at roll-call it learned to stand at attention with our Camp Leader, sometimes to be given a pat on the head by the officer of the day as the count was begun.

Then, an amazing discovery of a Pavlovian nature was made. Every time a piece of raw onion was placed on his nose, Bosco would defecate on the spot! This remarkable and hilarious reaction was at once put to good use. Next morning Bosco was in his accustomed place at the gate awaiting the entrance of the officer of the day for roll-call, but with one difference. He now faced backwards, bushy tail where his nose ought to have been. The gate opened, and in marched Pitblado with his escort of five soldiers, ready to start the count. A slice of onion was quickly administered to the unfortunate Bosco's nose, and on cue and with a rather fruity whump, a large soft turd hit the ground directly in front of the startled captain.

An epidemic of laughter broke out and the men struggled to keep faces straight. The contagion spread to the five soldiers, who had to wipe away tears of silent mirth as they accompanied the red-faced Pitblado on the rest of his round.

Bosco was banned from the compound at future roll-calls. Some wag remarked that he had been lucky to escape a visit to the cells.

15
Recreation

But still there were not enough outlets for the energies of the younger internees. Since not all could be accommodated in the work parties, the remainder of the actively inclined ones attempted to create their own entertainment. In the summer months several different activities would take place at the same time. At one end of the cramped compound an exercise group performed callisthenics; at another boxing matches took place in an improvised ring, and at another queues formed for a game of ping-pong. All this was done with equipment generously provided by the War Prisoners Aid of the YMCA. Some of the younger prisoners became obsessed with the maintenance of physical fitness, and at times the compound had the appearance of a training field, with groups of men performing all kinds of exercises with the utmost determination and vigour. The more dedicated amongst them set up organised physical culture groups with daily routines, with all of this holiday camp-type activity taking place under the grim shadow of barbed wire and the machine-gun emplacements at each end of the camp. Although they were not allowed to loiter by the guards, at weekends the sight of all this activity would be enjoyed by the good citizens of Montreal strolling on the bridge above.

Boxing was a favourite sport, and the few pairs of boxing gloves eventually supplied to the camp by the YMCA were in constant use. The uncrowned champion of the prisoners was Bruno Castellani, an extremely unrepresentative type from the seamens' group, Castellani came from Mestre, the port of Venice where he was rumoured to have embarked under mysterious circumstances. Some spoke of the killing of a police informer there, while others mentioned vague stories of Communist activities. An air of brooding mystery surrounded the man. But whatever his background, he was certainly not a typical sailor. Well read and intelligent, he spoke scathingly and openly against the Fascist regime in Italy. He taunted the lurking Malusa about his little black book and was supremely confident that his physical strength could cope with any threat from the Fascist groups who eyed him with open hostility.

He was a fine boxer and would spar with anyone regardless of weight or size. Only two men in the camp could extend Bruno Castellani. One was Tontini, the hard man from the East End of London and the other was Gerry Moscardini from the notorious Garscube Road in Glasgow. The former had served his fighting apprenticeship with the gangs of London and the latter was well versed in fending off the thugs and drunks who infested the area where his family's fish and chip shop flourished. Expert though they both were in the art of self-defence, they could make little impression on the powerful, and at times savage, Castellani.

It was at this point that the despised Moramarco gained the grudging respect of the camp. Since his downfall at the time of the mutiny the tall handsome gigolo had kept himself very much to himself. The loss of all personal privileges had meant that he had to rub shoulders with the lower orders of the camp, and this he did with a calculated disdain intended to show that in no way did he belong to the common herd. Vain and self-centred though he was, he nevertheless possessed a curiously likeable naiveté and on the rare occasions when he relaxed enough to take part in camp activities, he could be an excellent companion. Although he never participated in the work parties, he maintained his superb physique with daily exercises, and as the resentment of being treated in the same way as everyone else wore off, he began to take part in group sporting events.

He took a keen interest in the boxing matches and finally, after days of urging, was persuaded to put on the gloves with an eager Castellani. Moramarco stood for everything Castellani hated and resented. The man had good looks and obviously considered himself a cut above the common man. He was used to privilege and came from a social group that Castellani, with his Communist leanings, disliked intensely.

The two men presented a striking contrast as they stood ready to do battle, surrounded by almost the entire camp who had come hoping to see the proud Moramarco humbled. Castellani was a short and powerfully built man with strong sloping shoulders and well-developed forearms, whilst Moramarco, beautifully proportioned, stood almost a head taller and had about a 14lb-advantage in weight. Castellani started viciously, throwing punches from all angles in an attempt to make short work of his opponent, but Moramarco, showing the athleticism which had earned him a place in the Italian Olympic team, gave a fine exhibition of boxing, took all the punishment his adversary could throw at him and fought Castellani to a standstill, emerging after ten rounds of hard fighting as the undisputed points winner of the contest. He was given an enthusiastic ovation by the spectators, earning a rather sheepish handshake from the well-beaten Castellani as well.

On one occasion two brothers named Servignini from the London area, as typical a couple of cockneys as one could hope to meet with not a single word of Italian between them, and who hoped to make a profit by keeping a book on the event, came up with the idea of organising a race around the compound. The race was to be of ten laps, which represented a distance of about a mile. The winning prize was to be five dollars, and since this sum represented more than four weeks pay at the going rate of 20 cents a day, this was a prize well worth winning.

Sixteen runners entered for the event, scheduled for three weeks ahead, and they embarked on an intensive period of training, which gave the prospective punters ample opportunity to study the form of the participants. Great attention was paid to diet. All fatty and starchy foods were eschewed, and foods of choice were willingly provided by an enthusiastic kitchen as the contestants strove to bring themselves to a peak of fitness for the race.

But one of the entrants had his own methods of training. Fernando Barsi was the Glasgow-born son of an Italian father and Scottish mother, who neither spoke nor understood a single word of Italian and was the least likely candidate for internment that could be imagined. He had inherited his mother's blonde colouring and spoke English with such a thick Glasgow accent that on one occasion I had to act as English interpreter between Fernando and the Cambridge-educated Martinez! Barsi would have been certain of freedom had he elected to return to the UK at the time of Paterson's visit, but since this would have meant facing the dangers of an

Atlantic crossing with almost certain conscription into the army on arrival, he had elected to sit the war out in Camp S.

Sit out was the exact phrase, for he made full use of the potential for doing nothing offered by the camp. He ate well, did as little as possible and worked only when necessary to earn a few cents to feed his addiction to the O'Henry chocolate peanut bars on sale in the canteen, for as some men crave tobacco, Barsi craved O'Henrys. He was also exceptionally fond of food, a trait which at one time earned him a day in the cells which, according to the brass plaque now adorning them, was reserved for dangerous Nazi and Fascist prisoners.

During one mealtime Barsi had occasion to go back to the service counter at the kitchen for some reason or other and immediately encountered a problem. He spoke no Italian, so there was no possibility of any form of verbal contact between himself and the sailors who attended to the catering side of the camp at that time. Not that Barsi's lack of Italian would have mattered that much, because the kitchen staff spoke no proper Italian either, so without a working acquaintance with the thick Calabrese-Sicilian-Sardinian dialects in which the sailors conversed, no understanding would have been possible between them. Frustrated at the lack of response to his requests, Barsi, not lacking in physical courage, grabbed one of the cooks by the throat who defended himself by seizing a meat cleaver with which he attempted to decapitate the enraged Barsi. A confused mêlée ensued, with Barsi's friends and the rest of the kitchen crew joining in. The altercation was stopped only by the prompt intervention of Camp Leader Martinez, who solved the problem by persuading Barsi to retire to the cells for a day for his own protection and until the irate sailors could be placated and order restored.

Despite his natural indolence Barsi was immensely strong and fit, so when the chance of winning five dollars arose, he was stirred into entering for the race. After all, five dollars would buy a lot of O'Henrys at five cents a bar. His training method had no frills: plenty of raw eggs and peanut bars washed down with draughts of milk, a lot of rest, and one slow jogging mile round the track each morning. He explained to all who could understand him that he was conserving his energies for the great day.

That day dawned and the atmosphere in the camp was electric. Betting had been very heavy, with Agostini (who was later to attempt

RECREATION

an escape by swimming the St Lawrence),[1] a clear favourite, myself a near second and Barsi running an outsider at 50-1. Everyone in the camp, together with the guards outside, had turned out for the spectacle. To give the runners maximum room at the edge of the compound, the onlookers had grouped mainly in the centre in the manner of the spectators at the *Palio*, the spectacular medieval horse race which takes place each year in the Piazza del Campo of Siena, and excitement was at high pitch as the start of the race was signalled.

Much as expected, Agostini took the lead in magnificent style, with the rest of the field hard pressed to keep at his heels and with Barsi lagging far behind as the race progressed. Ten laps of the circuit had to be negotiated, and we concentrated on our exertions with no clear idea of how many laps there were to go. Then, over the roar of the cheering crowd, the timekeeper signalled for what he had counted as being the last lap.

Agostini was far ahead of the field as he crossed the finishing line and he was immediately surrounded by a crowd of admirers. The other runners slackened pace and stopped behind him. All except Barsi, that is, for he had counted the laps correctly and realising that the timekeeper had made a mistake, continued on his steady lope around the track. Agostini and the rest of us had completed only nine laps and although the race was restarted after a few seconds of noisy confusion, Barsi was too far ahead to be caught, and he finished the race a controversial winner. A near riot ensued as scores of punters clamoured for a re-run, but the result stood, with Barsi assured of a plentiful supply of O'Henry bars for some time to come. A rank outsider had won and the Servignini betting consortium had made a handsome profit on the event!

Football was a favourite sport. The YMCA provided football equipment for the prisoners, and the compound on Saturdays was reserved for soccer matches With the constant sub-zero temperatures of the winter months, such activities were not possible, but with the onset of freezing weather a section of the compound would be flooded with water, and the area then served as an ice rink until the spring thaw. Ice hockey teams flourished and the occasional encounter with teams from the soldier-guards were eagerly looked forward to and vociferously supported. These could sometimes be

---

[1] See chapter 18

rough and vengeful affairs. The soldiers on guard at the camp would be changed every few months. At times we would have French-Canadians on guard, and on other occasions English-Canadians would take over. The matches with the French would be reasonably good natured but the English on the other hand, did not think much of the wops and matches with them could be mutually vicious affairs. During one particularly nasty encounter blood flowed on both sides, and the ice hockey encounters were soon outlawed by order of the commandant.

For the less energetic and more intellectually minded, a series of study groups were set up by the prisoners themselves. With the aid of text books and writing material supplied by the YMCA, and with the wide fund of knowledge and expertise to be found among the prisoners, classes in many subjects were organised to which the Jewish group contributed in no small measure. The organiser of these intellectual activities was Romeo Capitanio of Stockwell in London. Born in Vienna of Venetian parents some 30 years before, his early education had been in Venice. At the age of ten the family had emigrated to Britain. His father, a stone sculptor, had become much in demand in sculpting the imposing statues which at the time decorated many of the bank and office blocks being erected in the financial heart of London.

After a short depressive illness Capitanio senior committed suicide, leaving the young Romeo as the sole support of his distraught mother and young sister. A serious and diligent young man, Romeo devoted all his time to the family, yet managed to obtain a BL degree at London University whilst furthering his career in the foreign exchange department of the London branch of the Credit Lyonnaise Bank. He was completely bilingual and possessed an honesty of character and sense of duty which at times bordered on the pedantic. He had no political views of any kind, and why such a kind and honest person should have been considered a threat and interned is difficult to understand. His help and encouragement was always available in any activity which would benefit his fellow prisoners and it was through his efforts that so much learning material was given to the camp by the various Red Cross organisations. With his help many programmes were set up.

For instance, Barocas, assistant to the Astronomer Royal at Greenwich Observatory set up classes in astronomy. These were

RECREATION

given in English and consisted mainly of a series of talks on the nature of the stars and planets. He was a captivating speaker, and his lectures were always very well attended. Carlo Treves, a small, dapper Professor of Chemistry at Rome University who had fled Italy at the time of the passing of the anti-Semitic laws in 1939 and who, it was rumoured, had masterminded the chemical warfare resorted to in the invasion of Abyssinia, gave classes in elementary chemistry. Tagiuri, the young lawyer, gave several talks on law, with constant repetition of the illegality of the transportation of civilian internees across military zones. Talks on navigation were given by Festa, a Fascist first officer of one of the merchant ships. Caproni, a ship's engineer, showed a remarkably deep knowledge of the works of Dante, and with the help of a large volume of the poet's work supplied by the International Red Cross kept his well-attended class going for the full three years of the camp's existence.

Furthermore, Gottlieb, another member of the Jewish group, started classes on chess. The game became very popular, and soon a corner of the recreation hut was reserved for this pastime. Father Roffinella set up classes in English. The first of these was a basic introduction to the language much frequented by the literate element in the sailor group. The second class was on the history of English literature for the benefit of the English-speaking section of the camp. Father Frizzero, himself a student in his colleague's elementary class, organised Italian study groups. These were well attended both by some of the sailors and by the Scots English fraternity.

Classes were run with greater or less ability on many subjects, with anyone who had any sort of interesting knowledge to impart being asked to come forward and share their learning with the rest of the camp. Giovanni Valente, a young restaurant owner from Newcastle, actually gave lessons in the theory of how to drive a motor car, all done with diagrams. So useful were these lessons that in the year after my release I was able, after only a few moments of tuition, to take control of a motor car and drive in traffic with the theory learned in these classes.

George Martinez set up a course in advanced mathematics attended by Capitanio and an obscure Londoner with the improbable name of Amatruda. His class started off with close on a dozen students, but dwindled off to the above two as the lessons became ever more difficult. In the land of the blind the one eyed man is king, and I too set up a class, in German, my own learning of which is narrated in another chapter of this book. I was able to teach my class learnedly with lessons that I had memorised only the previous day! The War Prisoners Aid of the Canadian YMCA took a keen interest in these classes and actually arranged for correspondence courses to be undertaken with the University of Saskatchewan in some of the subjects. I participated in the scheme with a course in German for almost a year and permitted myself a chuckle at the wry thought that it had taken a world war and imprisonment to gain me access to higher education.

As we had some of London's best chefs, Camp S boasted of a kitchen that was the envy of the soldiers. Although supplied with exactly the same rations as ourselves, they had to be content with the unimaginative and stodgy product of their army kitchens. Their officers fared infinitely better, however because they had the services of Sampietro of the Café Royal in their mess and the cuisine was probably unequalled in Montreal.

Christmas 1942 was approaching, and the commandant in charge of the camp was now Colonel Duvar, a genial English-Canadian under whose command relations between prisoners and guards had never been better. One evening after a particularly enjoyable meal, the colonel was taken by an idea. Why should his men not have a good Christmas dinner that year, prepared by the chefs in the camp? The Camp Leader George Martinez agreed that the idea was excellent and that no doubt, in exchange for the chef's services, an extension of this Yuletide spirit should offer some benefit to his men also. The word 'spirit' was interpreted literally and it was agreed that because it was Christmas wine would be provided at the dinner for both captors and captives.

Christmas day duly arrived. Mass was said by Father Roffinella, and then the men assembled for the long-awaited banquet. The chefs had worked well, and the excellently cooked traditional Christmas dinner was washed down with copious draughts of a strong dark wine of unknown origin. This arrived in five litre jugs in quantities which gave each man about two litres of the stuff, and the effect on men who had not tasted alcohol for years was startling. There was not a sober soul in the camp. The inebriation of the prisoners was matched only by that of the guards, who had enjoyed identical fare in their own quarters. By the end of the day guards and prisoners both were in the middle of a good-natured binge, with the men and their captors roaming the area in groups, arms entwined and differences forgotten in a haze of good food and bad alcohol. Not an officer was seen for two days, and any prisoner so minded could have wandered unhindered from the confines of the camp. The camp also had a fair sprinkling of good musicians and singers, and with the arrival of a selection of musical instruments gifted by the Red Cross and YMCA, a very good little orchestra was formed by the prisoners. Zeno, one of the Jewish group, was a fine violin player. Armando Esposito, a wine merchant from the Tottenham Court Road in London, played excellent guitar, and in addition to his culinary skills, Sampietro was a fine accordionist.

These three formed the nucleus of the so-called Orchestra Camp S, whose recitals were eagerly looked forward to by the prisoners, and in the summer the soft velvet nights on the St Lawrence were made nostalgic by the sound of melodies and songs rising from the courtyard of the camp. The music would range from the soft *O Sole Mio* and *Santa Lucia* of the sailors, through *The Bonnie Banks of Loch Lomond* of the Scottish contingent, to the harsher marching songs of the handful of Afrika Korps PoWs, who, as will be seen later, occasionally lodged in the camp. It was from them that we first heard the haunting *Lili Marlene*, the song that had been adopted by both the opposing armies in the North African Desert.

Towards the end of 1942 Canadian radio recorded a programme in the camp to be broadcast to Italy on the BBC Overseas War Service. This consisted of musical selections interspersed with messages to families back home. I was asked to act as compere for the programme, which I did with great gusto. Malusa's black book was worked overtime recording the names of all participants in the affair, which was branded as British propaganda by the Fascists. It has to be admitted that their description of that broadcast was probably an accurate one!

16
Health

In any situation where 400 men are crammed together as they were in Camp S, the maintenance of reasonable health can present problems. Fortunately, adequate nutrition was not one of them, for the rations issued to us were plentiful and of good quality. Personal hygiene was of the utmost importance, and fortunately this was not difficult to maintain. Washing and latrine facilities were far from generous, but by staggering their use each prisoner could maintain a high standard of cleanliness if he so wanted. There were, however, the naturally indolent and the mentally depressed who took no pride or interest in personal hygiene and who, if permitted to by their neighbours, would have allowed their personal cleanliness to deteriorate to unacceptable levels. Crudely put, when anyone began to stink of stale sweat and urine to the extent of disgusting their immediate neighbours, a barrage of colourful invective would usually be enough to shame them into taking a shower and washing their underclothes. But depression and apathy sometimes were too great a barrier to overcome, and there were times, happily very few, when the occasional prisoner had to be forcibly stripped and scrubbed under a shower by his unsympathetic companions.

A small room on the second floor of the fortress was set aside by the authorities to serve as hospital quarters. The room contained four single beds which boasted of proper bed sheets and pillows, a small desk and a medicine cabinet the contents of which consisted of a few bottles of aspirin tablets, some bandages with sticking plaster and a bottle of disinfectant. The person in charge was Dr Rybekil, a mysterious internee from northern Italy who was promptly called 'Dr Aspirin', after the only medication he was able

HEALTH

to prescribe for any ailment no matter how serious. Nothing was known about his background; his only contact was with the Jewish contingent, and he left the camp with them after Paterson's visit.[1]

His place in charge of the aspirin bottles and sticking plaster was taken by a young teenage boy by the name of Peter Maiolani who had had some training in first aid as a troop leader in a Boy Scout group in London. The well being of the camp did not suffer as a result of Rybekil's departure; his function had been simply that of referring obviously serious cases of illness to the Canadian Medical Officer, who theoretically should have arranged for proper treatment.

Fortunately the general health of the camp was good; apart from a trail of cuts and bruises and aches and sprains, few serious health problems arose in the camp. At the beginning of the first winter, as temperatures began to plummet below zero, Peter Pioli, a young man in his twenties from the Manchester area, came down with a wracking cough, the persistence of which forced an unwilling visit to Dr Rybekil. The doctor, on noting other disturbing symptoms, referred the patient to the medical officer. The diagnosis was tuberculosis for which treatment in proper hospital surroundings was necessary. Also necessary was complete quarantine, for in the cramped and unsanitary conditions of the dormitories, which during the winter nights were completely sealed to exclude the bitter cold, the disease could have spread like wildfire.

So, in the middle of a bitter Canadian winter, with night temperatures of minus 15 degrees and worse, an isolation tent just large enough to accommodate a camp bed was erected in a corner of the compound, and here the unhappy Pioli spent about three months. During the day he could be seen, a forlorn, blanket-wrapped Kafkaesque figure gazing at the bleak compound through the smoke of a wood burning stove which had been provided for heating. At night he lay motionless in his cot, apathetically gazing at the flickering sparks of the burning wood. Food was brought to him three times a day by volunteers and his use of the toilet facilities restricted so as not to make contact with the rest of the prisoners. These nightmarish conditions lasted for about three months. One morning the tent and its occupant had vanished, gone to a proper treatment centre, the camp was told. Nothing more

---

[1] See chapter 13

was heard of Pioli. Why he was not immediately removed from the camp on discovery of his disease was a mystery, but to have subjected a sick man to the misery of such conditions for such a time was disgraceful.

Paul Saulino was a young glove maker from the Midlands of England, who one day began to walk with a slight limp. This did not seem to affect his activities, for he was as agile as ever, joking with his companions about the fact that his right leg seemed to be growing longer as the days went by. The difference in length became very noticeable and his condition was brought to the attention of George Martinez, who asked the medical officer to examine the prisoner. The Canadian Officer refused to accept the fact that Saulino's leg was growing in length, and viewed the claim as some sort of practical joke, and he brusquely dismissed the unhappy prisoner. But the leg was indeed growing in length, and the concerned Martinez reported the matter to a Red Cross official who some weeks later was making a rare inspection visit to the camp. As a result of this complaint Saulino was immediately taken to a Montreal hospital where his leg was amputated at the hip, and a large tumour removed from the joint. Had the condition been treated at the outset the amputation might well have been avoided.

Although the general hygiene of the camp was good, on one occasion contaminated food must have been served out from the kitchen, for one summer morning the usual patient wait for a lavatory seat became a mad and uncontrollable stampede as a sudden wave of dysentery hit us. No one seemed to escape — the lavatory facilities were literally swamped; every available utensil, no matter how improbable, was put to use, and the compound was filled with miserable squatting men relieving themselves on the ground. The epidemic lasted for a day or so. The kitchen was completely cleaned out and disinfected and all areas in the camp had to be thoroughly hosed down and washed to get rid of the all-pervading stench of faeces. When all symptoms finally subsided the prisoners were placed on a diet of bread and milk for some days until normality returned.

One had to keep occupied all day long or else run the risk of falling into depression and melancholy. Nevertheless some prisoners spent all their time literally just eating and sleeping

HEALTH

and these were the ones most prone to the psychological problems created by the Camp S environment — one which would have been a fruitful field of investigation for any psychiatrist, with its overtones of a PoW camp, thousands of miles away from the point of origin of the civilian prisoners.

The soldier PoW at least has the consolation of knowing that he has served his country and that his imprisonment is but an extension of his military service, thus rendering his plight emotionally more bearable. Moreover, he is still subject to military discipline with the stabilising effect of an ordered existence. The convicted criminal serving a sentence in prison knows that he is expiating his sins against society by a fixed period of incarceration and that having broken the law he has merited his sentence. The civilian internees of Camp S, however, had no such factors to help them cope with their situation.

We were there because of an accident of birth and because of circumstances completely outwith our control, with no fixed end to our confinement in sight. For most of us too there was the added frustration of having been imprisoned by the society in which we had lived most, if not all, of our lives and all these emotions readily gave rise to feelings of paranoia, anger, despair and depression. The priests played a very important part in the maintenance of morale in the camp and in the counselling of those most afflicted by depression and despair. Mass was said each morning in the recreation hut before breakfast, and the ceremony was invariably well-attended. Then the priests would spend the rest of the day mixing with the prisoners, quietly taking note of the more morose and depressed ones so as to be able to direct their spiritual help to those most in need.

Emotional tensions were always high. The unchanging nature of camp life, the tantalising views of the city across the river through the barbed wire; the sight of free civilians on the bridge above; the uncertainty of the future — all these factors contributed to a general lack of morale among the men. These tensions no doubt played a part in a manifestation of mass hysteria which took place during the summer of 1941.

Roberto Sangari was a tall, dark and flabby figure of a man. Untidy and unkempt, his physical appearance was unhealthy and repulsive, with skin blotched and covered in tiny sores and deep-set Svengali-like eyes. Apart from the fact that he was Jewish and that he spoke good English with a heavy southern Italian accent, nothing was known of his background. Wild rumours circulated about him and his appearance, and the fact that Dr Rybekil was his only friend in the camp further fuelled the conjecture surrounding him. He participated in none of the camp activities, was excused all work duties, ate alone at the refectory table, was avoided by the prisoners, and spent the whole of the day sleeping in his bunk.

One summer afternoon the camp assembled for six o'clock roll-call. The day had been hot, sunny and humid, with temperatures soaring into the 90s and the men stood uncomfortably in the compound awaiting the entrance of the inspection party. Many had been out on work parties all day, so were tired and hungry, and we were all anxious to have roll-call over as quickly as possible. The minutes ticked by, the dust scuffed up by 400 pairs of feet hung low in the motionless air, and the humidity and heat seeming to become ever more oppressive.

Suddenly there was a strangled shout from the middle of group five. There stood Sangari, a hand raised with finger pointing to the sky, wheeling and turning and shouting as if to draw attention to something above. He turned slowly in circles with choked and strangled screams coming from his contorted mouth. His raised arm stabbed up in a series of punching motions, he spun round faster and faster, and uttering hoarse screams, collapsed and crumpled to the ground in a contorted mass. He lay there for a moment, uttering animal noises with vomit and saliva dribbling from his mouth, his jerking legs kicking up little spurts of dust.

A few seconds passed, and then, as though a giant scythe had been wielded amongst them, men began falling to the ground. Spreading out from Sangari's body like ripples in a pond, a mass fainting fit seized the camp, until a carpet of bodies lay on the ground. I stood, seized with nausea and revulsion at the sight of Sangari's gyrating and twitching body on the ground. I was aware, as if in a dream, of Dr Rybekil ministering to the body on the ground and then I proceeded to be sick on the spot. Of the 400 men assembled, only about 100 remained standing, all in various stages of fright, nausea and surprise at the spectacle around them. The hysteria had spread to several of the guards on duty outside the barbed wire, for even there several uniformed figures had slumped to the ground. Slowly the unconscious men came to. The still body

HEALTH

of Sangari was carried to sick quarters under the supervision of Dr Rybekil and the shaken prisoners were dismissed after a very hasty inspection by the officer of the day.

The incident remained indelibly etched in my mind, and for years afterwards I would be plagued by recurrent sweat-drenched nightmares centred around Sangari's madness, which was later to be revealed as having been an epileptic fit.

17
Language

The year 1941 had dragged on. In February of that year the first contingent of the Afrika Korps landed in Africa and the series of see-sawing battles culminating in the defeat of Field Marshal Rommel at El Alamein began. In May, Addis Ababa fell to British troops, Haile Selassie was reinstated as Emperor of Abyssinia, and Mussolini's African Empire, so recently acquired, crumbled to dust with the last of the Italian army in Africa under the Duke of Aosta surrendering to the British at Karen in Eritrea.

In June Germany invaded Russia and it became obvious even to the most ardent right-wing prisoners that an Axis victory was by no means a foregone conclusion. Indeed, the certainty of an Allied victory dawned with the USA's entry into the war in December 1941. Strangely enough, all this made for a much more relaxed atmosphere in the camp. The extreme Fascists were no longer regarded with fear, the merchant navy officers relaxed control over their men, who as a result mingled more freely than ever with the so called *Inglesi*. Malusa and the threat of his little black book were now largely ignored, and the possibility of defeat in the war was openly discussed. Remarkably too, news of German reverses in the war, Luftwaffe losses over Britain, the sinking of the *Bismarck*, the defeat of the Afrika Korps, the losses at Stalingrad — all these were greeted with an almost cold indifference by the prisoners as if they were events unconnected with Italy's presence in the war. It was almost as if such news was of no concern to Italians.

Slowly the tensions created by the destruction of the radio lessened, and each group kept very much to itself, thus avoiding the possibility of friction and conflict. Then, to the general delight of the prisoners, a weekly cinema show was introduced to the

LANGUAGE

camp. This was an Army entertainment unit consisting of a 16mm projector with a supply of all the latest Hollywood productions, obtained for the camp through the good offices of the International Red Cross. Permission was given by the Camp Commandant for films to be shown once a week in the recreation hut, subject of course to the good behaviour of the prisoners.

The recreation hut bulged at the seams on the occasion of the first show, *Captains Courageous* with Spencer Tracy and Freddie Bartholomew. The audience, packed tightly into every available inch, sat and stood enraptured, for a short two hours, with the reality of their surroundings forgotten. The non-English-speaking section of the camp were not happy however, for the dialogue was meaningless to them, so I began the challenging and satisfying undertaking of doing a simultaneous translation of the films for the sailors. Approached by my little Sicilian sailor friend, Nardo, on their behalf, I drew up a petition asking for a second showing of each film for the benefit of the merchant seamen. This was agreed to and I sat surrounded by scores of sailors listening eagerly to my translation of the dialogue.

To five of the sailors in particular the cinema was a source of wonder and amazement. These were the crew of a fishing smack which had been fishing off the island of Ischia near Naples on the day of the outbreak of war. Sailing out of a fog bank they had come upon a surfaced British submarine which promptly made them prisoner, presumably in order to maintain the position of the submarine secret. Once back at Gibraltar they were transferred to a ship on its way home to Liverpool, where they were joined up with the *Ettrick* contingent for Canada. The captain of the submarine must have been a kind-hearted man, for he could just as easily have sunk them without trace.

It may seem incredible to believe now, but these five had never seen a cinema show, so remote were their villages of origin and so devoid of any form of outside entertainment were the lives they led in the Italy of 60 years ago. One in particular, Baldino by name, was particularly fascinated and his reaction at the first film show was quite remarkable. He prowled round the back of the screen to see if there was anyone behind creating the images in front and could not grasp the concept of the two dimensional quality of the picture, and strained to obtain other views of the images. Although Baldino was of average intelligence, a time traveller from the middle ages could not have been more mystified at this new marvel.

He became one of my best customers at the translation sessions, pushing his way to the front so as not to miss a word of the story and would pester me afterwards for detailed explanations of the plot. I took considerable pride in these translations. I tried to convey accurately in Italian the meaning of the dialogue as it unfolded and I found great satisfaction in the knowledge that the translations were very skilfully done. At that time Hollywood was producing many films of worth: screen versions of some of Dickens novels such as *David Copperfield*; biographies of great men of history such as *Abe Lincoln* and *Juarez*; period films such as *The Hunchback of Notre Dame* and romances of the *Lost Horizon* type, all of which gave excellent practise in simultaneous translation from good English into Italian. The pot-boilers of the day, the gangster films, the Westerns, and the musicals, were all very trite stuff, with dialogue so repetitive and banal that I could actually finish the actors words before they did. So I became somewhat proficient in the art of simultaneous translation, which led to an interesting time for me in the camp.

Towards the end of 1941 I was given orders to type out a special order of the day for the notice board. This was an enquiry as to whether there were any fluent German speakers who might wish to apply for a position as an interpreter. In a few months Camp S, henceforth to be known as Camp 43, was to become a transit camp for German Officers and NCOs captured in North Africa until their transfer to camps further west.

The request went unanswered, for the only person who had any knowledge of German was Arturo Fonti, once a waiter in the Hotel Adlon in Berlin, and whose vocabulary did not stretch beyond basic kitchen matters. He would never have been capable of the type of interpreting required. So I volunteered for the job, despite the fact that I knew no German. I announced myself to the authorities as a fluent, although somewhat rusty, German speaker. I was on perfectly safe ground, for there was no one to put me to the test, so in the absence of any other applicants I was given the job and immediately set to work.

Declaring myself in need of practise and revision I asked for a dictionary, a grammar and a reader, all of which were unquestioningly supplied, and for the next two months I devoted every spare hour of the day to concentrated study. Declensions, genders and verb forms were committed to memory by a process of constant repetition. Each day I added ten new words and all their forms to my vocabulary. The reading book provided was a German translation of *Salambo*, a novel by Flaubert, which dealt with the semi-fictional adventures of a Libyan prince at the time of Hamilcar, the father of Hannibal. I laboriously translated the first page of the book, and the form of each verb and noun until the meaning of the sentences became clear. At the end of ten weeks of feverishly intensive work I had acquired a vocabulary of some 1000 words, and was able to read and translate the rest of the pages without a great deal of difficulty. There was one very big problem though. Apart from the contact with the German PoWs on the *Ettrick*, I had never heard a word of conversational German spoken in my life, so I awaited with some apprehension the arrival of the first contingent of prisoners. That day duly arrived, and I stood at the side of Colonel Duvar ready to put my newly-acquired knowledge to the test.

Preceded by a jeep armed with a rear-mounted machine-gun, an army lorry rolled into the courtyard. It stopped, the tailgate slammed down and the six occupants jumped out at the prompting of their guards. Still in their sand-stained uniforms of the Afrika Korps, with characteristic peaked caps on their heads, the German officers stood stretching their limbs, turning their heads with curiosity to take stock of their surroundings.

Prompted by Duvar I nervously stepped forward, cleared my throat, and proceeded to deliver my well-rehearsed speech.

'*Sie sind jetzt*... you are now in Camp 43 in Montreal. This is a transit camp where you will remain until transportation is ready to take you to your permanent camp further west.'

The senior officer, a tall blond young captain, looked at me and then Duvar and let loose a stream of words in a rapid guttural accent. I did not understand a single word of it. I swallowed nervously, and ignoring Duvar's enquiring glance, said slowly in German.

'*Bitte, sprechen Sie langsam*... please speak slowly, I am an Italian internee and I have never heard German spoken. Please speak slowly and clearly.'

The astonished captain looked at me with an open mouth, and with relief I understood my first spoken German words.

'Mein Gott, Er spricht wie ein Buch.'[1]

In a very short time, by dint of spending as much time as possible with the German PoWs, and a continuing intensive study of the language, I became as fluent in German as I had originally claimed to be, and I eagerly awaited every new German arrival so as to put my newly-acquired skill to use.

I revelled in my duties, happy at the acquisition of a new language and I took intense interest in my conversations with these German soldiers who had actually fought in the battles which were constantly talked about and which had an important bearing on the length of time we might have to remain as prisoners.

The Afrika Korps soldiers all had one thing in common: the overwhelming certainty of a German victory and a completely sincere belief in the rectitude of their cause, which was, to hear them tell it, the liberation of Europe from Jewish capitalist imperialism and the winning back for Germany all territories stolen from her in the 1914-18 war. They were all fine young men with first-class technical educations and yet, as far as a knowledge of history was concerned, the equal in ignorance to the illiterate merchant seamen of Camp 43.

About six months into my career as an interpreter, I was summoned to Duvar's office and instructed to hold myself ready for an important occasion, the arrival of a major of the Afrika Korps who would be housed at Camp 43 for a few days. I stood slightly apart from Duvar, looking up with curiosity and admiration at the figure who had just alighted from an army vehicle. More than six feet in height and wearing his battle-stained Afrika Korps uniform with authority, Major Haecker of the 15th panzer group, with his upright bearing and haughty look, more than fitted the bill of a proud hard-bitten German officer. The set piece introduction was gone into, but now with a confidence born of frequent practise.

'You are in Camp 43. . .', I began my monologue. Haecker towered a full eight inches over me. He looked arrogantly over my head, slowly surveying the compound, '. . .to your permanent camp further west', I concluded.

'What is this place, and who are you?' responded Haecker. Ever the perfect interpreter, I translated for Duvar's benefit, who

---

[1] 'My God, he speaks like a book!'

replied, 'This is an Italian internment camp, and your interpreter is one of the prisoners here.'

Haecker's face grew slowly purple under his tan, and with the veins on his temples standing out, he choked out some words.

'I refuse to stay here, and I refuse to have an Italian as interpreter!' I duly translated. Duvar looked for a moment at his prisoner, then replied with a cutting edge to his voice.

'You tell him that he is nothing more than a prisoner and in no position to demand anything. If he wants washed and fed he's to do as he's told, and until he's ready to do so he can stand there and take root as far as I'm concerned.'

And with these words he wheeled round and marched briskly off. I took a great deal of pleasure in translating the words. The deflated major stood for a moment glancing around him, then realising the impotence of his position, stuttered, 'Very well, but only under protest' and was duly escorted off to his quarters.

That evening I received a call to present myself at the officers' mess. There, seated opposite one another across a handsomely set dinner table were the officers of two opposing armies, on the one side the slim and diffident Duvar, and on the other Haecker, still in his battledress, but now washed and shaved and in a mellower frame of mind. I sat myself down between them and for the next two hours, during which the officers did justice to a magnificent meal prepared by Sampietro, I engrossed myself in translating for the two men. The talk ranged from politics and military matters to music, art and philosophy and after the meal was over I felt that I had done an excellent job.

Translation is very often a matter of conveying the exact meaning of the spoken phrase, often by the use of paraphrase rather than a word for word translation. I felt that I had achieved this very successfully and the end of the evening, quite exhausted, I was dismissed with a polite thank you from Duvar and a barely perceptible nod from Haecker.

The next day, as always, I started with some light exercises followed by a mile-long, ten-lap run around the compound. Having barely started the first lap I found my path blocked by the huge figure of Haecker.

'You did a good job last night. What's your name and where did you learn to speak German?' After my answer there was a pause and then he continued.

'Do you want to know why I despise Italians?' and without waiting for a reply continued. 'During an action in the region of Bardia I was in command of five panzers, 250 Afrika Korps infantry and 200 Italians of the Trento division with their officers. Because of strategic considerations I had to retreat, but began to run short of fuel. I then ordered two tanks to be buried in the sand with their cannon facing the pursuing British, who were about ten miles behind us, and left the 200 Italians with orders to stand and defend the position as long as possible.

'I then continued the retreat with my own men hoping to regroup and refuel at a base about 15 miles further back. Had the Italians done their duty I would then have been in a position to inflict heavy casualties on the enemy with a counter attack. But what happened? As soon as the first English patrols appeared two hours later, the Italians raised a white flag and surrendered without firing a shot. The English were able to advance rapidly, outflanked my group and we were all captured. That is why I am a prisoner here today and that is why I despise Italians.'

I allowed a pause, then asked.

'Why did you not leave some of your own men to defend the position if it was all that important?'

'My men were too valuable to me. The Italians were expendable.'

There was no further conversation and I continued my run with the unspoken thought that the Italians had shown uncommonly good sense in the circumstances.

The major remained in the camp for nearly a week. His meeting with Duvar was not repeated, but occasionally he would seek me out for company and conversation. The war was sometimes discussed and strangely enough, unlike the junior officers of the Afrika Korps for whom I had previously interpreted, Haeker did not believe that Germany could now win the war.

On the day of his departure he pulled an Iron Cross from his pocket and tossed it to me with the words, 'Goodbye. You can have this, I have no further use for it.'

Traffic through the camp was not all one way. Small groups of Germans, most of them Jews, occasionally arrived at Camp 43 on their way back to freedom in the UK from German internment camps further west. Although most of these could speak English,

LANGUAGE

I would still be called upon to greet them and acquaint them with the rules of the camp. They were in the main professional people who had fled from Germany to avoid arrest by the Nazis and from them were heard incredulous tales of atrocities against Jews and political dissidents and of the existence in Germany of camps where such people were tortured and put to death. These stories were met with a great deal of scepticism. One tends to judge matters in the light of one's own experiences, and there were many in the camp who dismissed the refugees stories as nonsense.

Their stories were made less believable by their own behaviour. Almost to a man they did nothing but complain about everything that had happened to them since the outbreak of war. As far as Camp 43 was concerned nothing was right. The food was not to their satisfaction, their accommodation was not to their liking, they did not see why they should have to mix with soldiers who were their sworn enemies, and so on and so on ad nauseam. The consensus of opinion was that if the tales they told about Nazi camps were true, they should then consider themselves fortunate and privileged to be where they were.

But then of course their stories were only too true, as was revealed when the full horror of the Nazi death camps became known in the months after the defeat of Germany.

18
Escape

The possibility of an escape from the camp was a popular topic for fantasy and discussion amongst the younger and more adventurous among us, for in 1941 the USA was still neutral and therefore sanctuary there was theoretically possible. The story of Lt Franz von Werra and his incredible escape from Canada and eventual return to Germany had been told and retold in the Canadian PoW camps, reaching legendary status in the telling. It had inspired many would be fugitives.

Von Werra was a Luftwaffe fighter pilot shot down and captured in England in the early days of the war. After two abortive attempts at escape from prison camps in England he was sent to Canada in a prison ship, where he arrived in January of 1941. Whilst in transit from the ship to a PoW camp in Ontario he made a daring escape from a heavily-guarded train in the neighbourhood of Montreal. He then made his way for some 50 miles in the bitter cold to the US border, crossing the frozen St Lawrence in the process. This was an amazing feat. The night temperatures in that region can drop to 20 or 30 degrees below zero at that time of the year and Von Werra was far from warmly dressed, with only a light top coat over his Luftwaffe uniform.

Already exhausted by the long trek, he had to surmount the final barrier of a 50-yard section of swift water as yet unfrozen in the middle of the St Lawrence, which at that point was about 1000 yards wide. This he did by going back to the Canadian side of the river bank where he found a small rowing boat and dragged it over the rough ice to the stretch of open water, where he drifted on the current to the American side of the ice. He ploughed on due south through the snow and was lucky enough to find shelter in a barn a few miles inside US territory, where he was found half dead by a farmer the next morning. The police took him to the small border town of Ogdenburg and since the USA was still neutral at the time, they handed him over to the German consul in New York pending a review of his case. Although the Canadians could not ask for him back as an escaped PoW, he was charged with the theft of the rowing boat in an attempt to have him extradited on a criminal charge.

His escape hit the American newspaper headlines in a sensational manner. He became something of a glamour figure for the tabloid press, and much sympathy was showered on him, especially by the many German-American groups still active in the state of New York. To avoid possible extradition back to Canada he disappeared from his house custody at the German consulate, and with money presumably supplied by that office, began an epic journey back to Germany. Firstly he made his way to San Francisco, where he booked his passage on a Japanese freighter to Yokohama. From there he proceeded on to Manchuria, and since the German invasion of Russia was still some months in the future, he was able buy a ticket on the trans-Siberian railway to Moscow. Then he headed home to Berlin, where he was decorated with the *Deutches Kreuz*, the highest German military order of the Second World War, presented personally to him by Göring.

The Von Werra saga finally ended in December 1941 when the young airman was shot down and killed on the Russian front in the Moscow sector through which he had passed such a short time before. After the war a book was written about his exploits by the German writer Fritz Wentzel, which was translated into English, and made into a successful film *The One That Got Away*. His exploits had filled the US and Canadian tabloids for weeks, some of which filtered through to the prisoners clandestinely. There they were read and re-read by admiring prisoners who grouped together to plan hypothetical escape procedures, more for the sake of something to do rather than achieve freedom. After all, home to many of the prisoners was the very country that had put them behind barbed wire, any escape would have been quite simply an escape to nowhere.

Camp 43 was not an easy place to escape from. Although the military presence inside the camp was minimal, the outside security arrangements were very tight indeed. The barbed-wire fence at the front of the compound was under constant surveillance from the two machine-gun towers, and guards patrolled constantly to and fro in front of it. During the night the area was bathed in the glare of searchlights and the slightest movement in the compound would have been immediately noticed. We had been well warned that anyone seen there between lights out and reveille the next morning would be shot at and no one to date had been foolhardy enough to test the truth of that statement.

The rear of the fortress presented no opportunity whatsoever to any potential escapee. The back of the building was a blank wall behind which the ground rose steeply to another barbed-wire fence just as impregnable as the one at the front. Escape from one of the outside work parties was feasible, but then the problem of getting off the island would have to be surmounted. The only exit on foot was over the bridge and here too soldiers were much in evidence, with four sentry boxes placed at strategic points on the footpaths.

One day towards the end of 1941, a few weeks before the entry of the USA into the war, I was approached by George Martinez, who had just resigned from the position of Camp Leader. The news that he was giving up the job was greeted with dismay by the men, who felt that they were losing a champion in dealing with their captors. The reason for his resignation, divulged only to myself, was an honourable one. Martinez, together with Festa the ship's mate, was planning an escape from the camp and he did not want it to be said that he had taken advantage of his position or of the trust that the authorities had placed in him. Despite the great difference in our respective backgrounds, with me the son of poor Tuscan peasants and Martinez, the Cambridge-educated son of wealthy Neapolitan parents, a friendship had grown between us. This was based mainly on the fact that we shared middle-of-the-road political ideas and on that open and frank discussion of all issues was possible between us without dissimulation or fear of repercussions. Although tensions in the camp had lessened somewhat since the departure of the Jewish group and of the left-wing sympathisers, open discussion of the war and of politics was still not possible. Accusations of being anti-Italian and inclusion in Malusa's little black book would still be the fate of anyone who dared question Italy's role in the war or cast doubts on the eventual triumph of

Mussolini's forces. Under such circumstances it meant a great deal to have someone to talk to honestly and openly.

He explained his plan to me. During the summer a small workshop had been erected at the far end of the compound for the purpose of packing Red Cross bandages into large wooden crates for shipment to Halifax. The crates were put together by the prisoners in the old Ste Hélène Powderhouse building some distance from the fort and the bandages came from a small factory in Montreal. These were delivered by van to the workshop each week and once a week, always in the afternoon, four or five filled crates were taken from the camp by lorry to the railway station, there to be loaded on to a freight train for Halifax.

At the time Martinez approached me, work on the bandage programme had been in progress for about two months. The furore described in chapter nine had been forgotten, with some of the original objectors themselves taking part in the project, so attractive was the prospect of more work to break the monotony of camp life. Pay of 20 cents a day which could buy chocolates and cigarettes in the camp canteen was an added incentive. The plan was that on the day of the shipment of the crates, two of them would be emptied of bandages during the midday break when the workshop closed for one hour. Martinez and Festa would take the place of the bandages, be loaded on to the lorry and driven out of the camp. Once on the train, the two would break out of the crates and make their way to the USA. Since the crates were handled by prisoners as far as the train, the extra weight would be ignored and the escape should go undetected until evening roll-call and, with a bit of luck and laxity on the part of the guards, even beyond that.

My help was indispensable. The crates were never shipped to any set routine. The camp office was notified of the arrival of the lorry only on the morning of shipment, and only then would the crates be packed and sealed for departure. Because of my presence in the office I would know of these arrangements and could give access to the workshop at the lunch break with the spare keys kept in the office. The opening and unpacking of the crates, the disposal of the surplus bandages and the sealing of the crates with the men inside would be carried out by a sailor named Lardaro, a tall taciturn Sardinian who served as Festa's batman.

I listened with interest to the plan. I did not particularly like Festa and had few dealings with him apart from any camp business that might arise. He was a highly intelligent and well-read man, which made his bigoted and intransigent Fascist opinions all the more irritating to me. Whilst I did not openly flaunt them, my moderate political opinions were made quite plain to anyone who cared to ask, and yet Festa seemed at times to go out of his way to engage me in conversation which would inevitably lead to a difference of opinion. I learned later that my views had never been reported to Malusa and I suspect that deep down he recognised the validity of my arguments. It seemed that the idea of such an escape had originated with Festa, and since he spoke no English he had thought of Martinez as a possible collaborator in the scheme.

I found the escape plan exciting, so I thought for a moment. Life was boring, dull and repetitive. What the hell! Why not? Anything to break the monotony, and my enthusiasm grew as I listened. I began to analyse the plan. The encased men would need ventilation, I suggested. A tube connected to a few holes punched in the sides of the packing cases should suffice. One helper would not be enough to do all the work in the time available; the conspirators would need an extra man and so I proceeded to offer my services to an enthusiastic Martinez.

The plan was worked upon and perfected. Two sets of clothing minus the tell-tale red disc and stripe were prepared with the help of the willing camp tailor Barletta, who was also to be the protagonist in a later escape of sorts. The conspirators waited tensely for news of the next consignment of bandages to be announced. Finally one morning the workshop was alerted to prepare five crates for dispatch that day, so the plan swung into action. That same forenoon, under the supervision of the French-Canadian sergeant in charge of the workshop, the crates were neatly packed and labelled and on the stroke of midday the whistle blew for the noon break. The prisoners filed out, and the sergeant, behind them all, locked the door behind him. Five minutes later I opened the side door of the workshop with my duplicate set of keys and gave entry to my three companions.

We set to work quietly and efficiently. Quickly the lids of two of the crates were prised open and the contents of each emptied on the floor. Martinez and Festa squatted down, one to each case and were packed in tightly with piles of bandages. A cardboard tube was placed in the vicinity of their mouths, taped to the side of the crate, then holes punched in the wood for ventilation. Finally their heads were covered over with bandages and the crates sealed, leaving them indistinguishable from the three others awaiting the arrival of the lorry.

The sailor Lardaro and I had worked quickly and efficiently. Care had to be taken not to damage the lids of the crates particularly when closing them, but nevertheless there was ample time left for the disposal of the excess bandages left over by the volume of the two fugitives in the crates. A heavy snow fall had taken place during the night before, with deep drifts piling up in the narrow space between the hut and the fortress walls, so Lardaro and I gathered up the bundles of bandages, with the intention of throwing them out of a rear window for burial in the snowdrift. With difficulty, we prised open the window and the bandages were shoved through the gap, which we then tried to close. But the intense cold must somehow have affected the window sashes, for strain as we might, a two-inch slit remained open.

To my horror, as the two of us struggled to close this, I noticed through the front window the approach of the work shop sergeant and one other soldier, about to return to their post almost half an hour before their expected time. Lardaro and I were forced to leave the window as it was, and just managed to slip out through the side door five seconds before the entry of the sergeant.

One by one the prisoners drifted back to their place of work and the crates moved to a position near the door ready for loading into the transport. The window gap had gone unnoticed by the sergeant as he busied himself issuing orders to his prisoners, nor had he seen that two of the crates required a great deal of effort on the part of the handlers. It was only when the main door had closed behind the loaded lorry that he became aware of a cold draught behind him. He looked a bit puzzled as he noticed the open window, and his curiosity increased when he saw that the snow on the sill had been disturbed. The puzzlement gave way to an expression of downright disbelief as he forced the window open fully and caught sight of the piles of bandages blending into the whiteness of the snow outside.

The implication of all this did not sink in immediately however, so it was only after a few minutes discussion with a hastily-summoned officer that the obvious became clear. The prisoners were ordered to shift the crates from the lorry back into the workshop, and the lids were prised open. One by one, the heads of Martinez and Festa, red and sweating from the heat in the packing cases, popped out like jack-in-the-boxes and the two were marched off under armed guard. The obvious question arose — who had put the men in the boxes? Despite intensive questioning the two men refused to give an answer. The new Camp Leader, a dapper little Londoner by the name of John Conti, was summoned to the colonel's office. Unless the culprit or culprits gave themselves up, he was told, all privileges in the camp would be cancelled; the canteen would be closed and the weekly cinema show indefinitely withdrawn. I had no alternative. I conferred briefly with Lardaro. There was no point in both of us going to the cells and besides, a confession from me would satisfy the military as to the manner of entry to the hut and knowledge of timetables.

So the two men in the cells were joined by a third, and there we spent the next 30 days in the expiation of our sins. The punishment was to include restricted rations for the period, so it came as something of a surprise when the three of us emerged from the cells after a month with considerable gains in weight. This was entirely due to the ministrations of Father Roffinella, who visited the cells each day for the purpose of bringing us prayer and spiritual solace. His spiritual exhortations were accompanied by all kinds of delicacies from the kitchen which he smuggled in under his voluminous winter clothing.

In retrospect, the Martinez-Festa attempt to escape was dangerous and foolhardy. Bathed in perspiration from the heat generated inside the two cases, even if the two men had managed to break out of the crates, thus escaping death by eventual asphyxiation, they might well have frozen to death in the sub-zero weather of a Canadian winter. In years to come George Martinez and I were to reminisce over the affair, the memory of which had now been blurred by the passage of time. As far as Festa was concerned, patriotism and the desire to embarrass the authorities was probably the motivating force. Certainly as far as Martinez and myself were concerned it was simply for a bit of adventure, for the hell of it, and for the want of something better to do.

There was a curious epilogue to the affair. At the end of the war with Italy, Martinez was released in Montreal and worked for a spell as a draughtsman in the office of a certain Lt Goodswan, an officer with whom he had become friendly during his stay on Ile Ste Hélène.

One day some group photographs taken in the camp were produced and a figure in one of them was identified by Lt Goodswan as an informer who had betrayed the escape attempt to the camp authorities. No specific information had been given, he said to Martinez, only that an escape was to take place somehow from the workshop at some unspecified time in some unspecified way. This information explained the early return by the two soldiers to the hut, who presumably had been told to keep a special eye on the premises. The informer was a quiet, unobtrusive man from the south of England where he may well live to this day.

Another foolhardy attempt at escape had been made some months before by John Agostini, against whom I had run in the race around the compound. The hard-looking London-Italian who actually was a Soho bookie's 'runner' was a taciturn and uncommunicative loner who spoke no Italian and mixed with very few of the prisoners. He was looked upon suspiciously by the sailor group, who classified him as one of the most English of the *Inglesi*, but no one dared cross his path for on several occasions he had demonstrated the hardness of his fists in fights from which he had invariably emerged the victor.

Daily exercises and as much work as possible on the work parties kept him in magnificent physical condition which one day he decided to put to the test. Unnoticed by the half-dozen bored guards in charge of the work detail, he slipped away from the Powderhouse joinery shop where wooden crates were assembled. Then, crouching and running in the shelter of thick shrubbery, he arrived at the water's edge. At that point the river bank faced almost due south and was separated from the south shore by some 500 yards of swiftly flowing water. Stripping off his uniform and tying his boots around his middle, Agostini plunged into the St Lawrence and began to swim towards the faraway bank.

He had not realised how strong the current was, for despite his strength as a swimmer, his progress was slow and laboured and it took him almost an hour to arrive, completely and utterly exhausted, at the far side of the river. Resting a while to recover from his exertions, he began walking due south towards the US border which lay some 50 miles away, clad only in the wet underwear in which he had swum the river, until he came upon an isolated farmhouse building outside of which some clothing hung on a line. Pausing for

ISLE OF THE DISPLACED

a moment to make sure there was no one around, he stole a pair of jeans and a shirt, then proceeded on his way.

By this time Agostini's disappearance had been noted. A meticulous search of the island was put under way, and on the assumption that somehow the prisoner had managed to get over the bridge, the Montreal police were alerted and the escape announced over the local radio. In those days that part of Quebec was sparsely populated and he walked for miles without meeting a living soul until in the distance he could see a cluster of houses and by the roadside a sign with the name *La Prairie.* At the edge of this stood a little wooden church. Tired and hungry, Agostini walked into the building with the intention of resting a while, sat down on a bench, then noticed some people seated on the pew in front, awaiting their turn to enter a confessional. On a sudden impulse he moved forward and sat with them. His turn to enter came.

'Bless me Father for I have sinned, I am an Italian prisoner and I have just escaped from the camp on Saint Helene's Island. Can you help me?' This in a broad London accent probably barely intelligible to the French-Canadian priest who was hearing confession. Receiving no answer, Agostini repeated his words to the confessional screen and this time got a response.

'I assume you are a Catholic, therefore you must know that you are abusing the confessional. I will give you two minutes to leave this place, then I shall call the police.' The priest paused for a moment then continued. 'Where do you hope to go? What do you hope to achieve? I advise you to give yourself up, my son.'

Exhausted by the exertion of his swim and the miles of walking in the hot sun Agostini felt the strength drain from his limbs, rose slowly to his feet, stumbled out of the confessional, then sat wearily on the pew outside, all his energy gone.

A few moments later the priest came out, and seeing the powerfully-built young man slumped in the seat before him, stopped.

'Are you. . .?' and got a dispirited nod for an answer. Some time later, filled with sandwiches and coffee, the farewell and blessing of the priest ringing in his ears, he was escorted from the church house by two Canadian Mounted Policemen, who returned him by jeep to the gates of Camp 43, there to run the gauntlet of his companions' cheers on his way to the mandatory 30-day sojourn in the cells. Agostini had ultimately been strong enough to return alive; a lesser man would surely have drowned in the powerful currents of the St Lawrence.

George Barletta was a quiet, unobtrusive 30-year-old tailor from the Edinburgh district, where he had lived and worked since his arrival from Italy about 15 years before. A reserved and uncomplaining bachelor with few friends, he participated in few of the camp activities, expressed no political views, and went about his daily routine patiently awaiting the day of his release. He volunteered daily for the work parties, for he enjoyed the occasional hard physical labour involved in clearing shrubs and bushes, the felling of trees and the maintenance of the many paths and walkways on the island.

Because of his reputation as a quiet and willing worker who never gave trouble, Barletta was chosen daily for these work parties, and in time had got to know the geography of the island thoroughly. On one occasion he was given the task of clearing out a storage hut at the edge of a remote clearing, where he was left to his own resources by a trusting guard. He was told to join the main group of prisoners when summoned by the whistle which signalled the end of the shift.

In a corner of the hut, half-hidden under a pile of old workclothes and assorted lumber, Barletta came across a rusty old bicycle. The machine, though covered in dust and cobwebs, seemed in fair enough condition and he spent some time cleaning and oiling it with some lubricant which he found close by. The tyres seemed firm enough, so he began to pedal slowly and thoughtfully round the clearing, nursing the germ of an exciting thought which had just come into his head.

That night, putting his tailoring skills to work, he removed the broad red stripe from a pair of trousers and the red circle from the back of a jacket, and replaced them with patches of blue material so as to make a normal looking suit, then loosely stitched back the red prisoner patches into place. Next day, out with the work party again, he was assigned another solitary task. He waited until the guard was out of sight, stripped off the red markings, ran to the clearing where the bicycle had been left and proceeded to pedal casually towards the slip-road leading to the bridge. He waved to the guards on duty, and accelerated briskly up and over the huge structure towards the city across the river.

There he spent an idyllic morning, alternately pedalling and walking his bicycle along the broad Montreal avenues, drinking in the sights and sounds of freedom. Taking careful note of the passage of time, he made his way back to the river, pedalled on to the bridge towards the island, where he joined the slip-road down, waving cheerfully to the guards as he did so. Arriving back at his departure point in the clearing, he replaced the bicycle in the hut, fixed the red markings back onto his clothes, and minutes later, summoned by the assembly whistle, rejoined his group to be counted and escorted back to the camp. Next day he repeated the procedure. He explored a different part of the city, enjoying to the full the sensation of unhindered and unlimited movement, and took care to be back in time for the guard's count.

On the third day disaster struck. He had gone as far as the summit of Mount Royal, had sat a while at the base of the huge cross, admiring the view down over the city to the river and the bridge, until time dictated that he should be on his way back. He mounted the bicycle and pushed off, freewheeling down the gentle slope of the hill, then without any warning, his front wheel collapsed in a tangle of wire spokes and struts, throwing him heavily to the ground. Shaken but unhurt, he started off on foot towards the island, for with not a cent in his pocket to pay for any form of public transport he was left with a long walk back to the island, with no possibility of being on time for roll-call.

The guard in charge of the work party counted and recounted his prisoners, but at last had to accept the fact that he was a man short. The alarm was given, the guard at the bridge trebled, and news of the escape, together with a description of the fugitive, was given to the Montreal police. About two hours later a footsore Barletta arrived at the Jaques Cartier bridge, squared his shoulders, then began the long trek over the pedestrian walkway towards the island and on to the slip-road leading down to the fort.

He noticed the trebling of the guard, who took only casual notice of the pedestrian walking along towards the island, for their orders were to stop any one leaving the area, not going towards it. Barletta was soon back in his clearing, where the red markings were waiting to be replaced on his prisoners uniform. Up he marched to the fortress gates, rattled the bars and demanded entry of a startled guard who escorted him immediately to the officer in charge of the search. The latter listened somewhat sceptically to his tale of having fallen asleep under a bush and only just awakened; the scepticism turning to complete disbelief when the superimposed red markings on his clothes were noticed. So Barletta told the truth, although this too was rejected as being very improbable until the Montreal police reported finding a damaged bicycle on the slopes of Mount Royal.

Whilst the episode could hardly be classified as an escape, it did earn him the acclamation and respect of his fellow prisoners. . . together with the usual 30 days in the cells.

19
O'Connor

One morning in early 1941 a new face appeared. J O'Connor Lynch had arrived. A soft-spoken Canadian of Irish descent, O'Connor Lynch (we never knew his Christian name) was a civilian employed by the army to act as interpreter for the Italian-speaking prisoners and as censor of the mail for all the camp. He was a precise little man of about 35 years of age with sleek black hair and he sported a neatly trimmed black goatee beard. He spoke fluent Italian and had an all embracing knowledge of Italy which he had acquired during a six year sojourn there in the early 1930s. He was an artist by profession and his six years in Italy had been spent studying the art and language of the country. He was also a passionate art collector, and his time in Italy had also been put to good use in acquiring for a modest outlay a collection of paintings the value of which was to grow enormously in later years.

He mingled freely in the camp, surprised that so many of the prisoners spoke no Italian, and spent a great deal of time in conversation with individual prisoners, questioning them closely about their backgrounds. There was much speculation as to his motives in mixing so freely with the inmates, but since he formed part of the Establishment it was generally accepted that he could be up to no good. He was treated with suspicion and reserve by the *Inglesi* as a result.

Strangely enough the sailors unreservedly accepted O'Connor, for here was a man who knew their country, even sometimes their native towns and villages, and spoke their language well. Furthermore their position was clearly defined unlike many of the civilian prisoners. They had no family connections in Britain or desire to return there and so they had no reason to create a good impression with the authorities, as might have sometimes been the case with the civilians. There was no need for them to dissimulate in any way with him, and O'Connor's frequent visits were welcomed as an occasion for meeting someone from the outside with whom they could talk freely.

One of the greatest consolations in the camp was the receiving of mail and parcels from home and these were the highlights of the prisoner's life. Unlimited receipt of letters was allowed, with outgoing mail limited to two per month per man. Family letters would be read and re-read and were treasured as a lifeline to an existence to which we one day hoped to return. The letters which O'Connor delivered to us had all been opened and read by him, for very often a delivery would be followed by solicitous enquiries about some piece of family news contained in the mail. All his enquiries were prefaced by a nervous little cough which came to be recognised as the overture to some personal enquiries. Each prisoner to receive a letter would be spoken to first in Italian, whether he knew that language or not, and then by number and not by name. His *'Buon giorno, numero ottanta sette, c'è una lettera per te'* [1] or whatever the number of the prisoner happened to be, became a catchphrase in the camp. I received a fair amount of mail each week from my parents and friends in Glasgow and at first I resented O'Connor's polite questions about my family and personal circumstances, always presaged by the introductory cough. With time, however, I came to realise that no ulterior motive lay behind the man's curiosity but merely a genuine desire to get to know us all better.

Because of my job in the office, I came into daily contact with him and slowly a cautious friendship developed between us. The relationship was fuelled by shared interests in art and literature which had been recently aroused in me by the many books sent to the camp by the Red Cross and by my attendance at the classes on Dante given by the ship's engineer, Emilio Caproni. O'Connor had to be careful not to give the impression of fraternisation in his contact with the prisoners, so often I would be called to his office, ostensibly to assist in translation work, but in reality to continue with some interesting conversation touched upon during his official tours of the camp. He was an urbane and civilised man, really more at home

---

[1] 'Good morning number 87, there is a letter for you.'

in the company of the variety of personalities to be found amongst the prisoners than in that of his army employers, and his two year stint in the camp contributed much to the morale of the prisoners.

As only natural under the circumstances, and second only to the progress of the war, one of the main topics of conversation was sex. Long-past amorous exploits would be told and retold with great embellishment, and there was hardly a bunk without its quota of pin-ups, running the gamut of every available pose of Betty Grable, Alice Faye and Rita Hayworth, together with a bevy of lesser-known Hollywood beauties.

The great lover and raconteur of the camp was Gerry Capaldi. To hear him tell it, in days gone by in London, he had been the Lothario of the West End. He was the name-dropper par excellence. According to him, his amorous exploits had spanned the social spectrum from waitresses through film starlets to the aristocracy. No doubt he had had some form of contact with the girls who peopled his imagination, for his job as a waiter at Gennaro's in Soho would certainly have brought him into contact with many attractive women, even if only to serve them the soup. Capaldi's Walter Mitty imagination provided the spark for the stories he wove round these lovely creatures from another life long ago. Nevertheless the prisoners listened with great good humour and complete disbelief to his tales while punctuating them with the inevitable string of ribald remarks that was to be expected in such company.

Then one day a letter arrived for me. Delivered as always by the urbane O'Connor, it had been slit open and read, but wonder of wonders, it bore a Canadian stamp and a Montreal postmark! For us the city across the river possessed an almost mystical quality. It represented freedom, civilisation, theatres, cinemas and. . . pretty girls: things which belonged to a distant past. The city was a Shangri La to be dreamt about and yearned after, and here was a letter to me which had actually been posted there.

'*Buon giorno numero otta*nta *sette, c'è una lettera per te.*'

Then in English, 'You're a lucky man, number 87. Your girlfriend has come to Montreal', and he moved off, leaving me to stare in amazement at the familiar handwriting on the envelope. How on earth could Dorothy have posted a letter in Montreal? Could she actually be there? I opened it with eager fingers and the mystery unfolded.

Dorothy had been my girlfriend back in pre-war days in Glasgow. The family restaurant was near Sauchiehall Street, within a stone's throw of the Pavilion and Empire theatres and was much frequented by many of the variety artists popular in Glasgow then. Dave Willis ate his fish suppers there. Tommy Morgan enjoyed his McCallums there, (as an ice-cream with raspberry sauce was called) and GH Elliot, the 'Chocolate Coloured Coon' of Lily of Laguna fame, had his ritual two poached eggs on toast and pot of tea in our Savoy Café before his evening performances in the neighbouring Pavilion.

But most glamorous and desirable of all to me were the luscious Bluebell chorus girls who would stop at the café for supper on their way to the theatrical lodging houses in the area. The most attractive of the girls as far as I was concerned was Dorothy D., a pretty young dancer from Preston. My affection was reciprocated, and during the Christmas panto seasons and yearly summer shows, Dorothy and I began to drift euphorically towards the idea of marriage, to the unconcealed dismay of our respective families. 'Sure Joe, Dorothy's a nice girl, but why don't you find a nice Italian girl for yourself?' And my mother would go into the familiar hand-wringing bout of lamentation about local girls which had not changed throughout the years. 'And not even a Scottish girl. . . but English!'

In parallel fashion, but with English reserve, Dorothy's family was politely frigid when I was introduced to them in Preston. 'Oh yes Dorothy. . . he's a nice chap, but he's an Italian!'

The situation was resolved by Mussolini's declaration of war. Dorothy went her way with the Bluebell troupe, I was interned and there the romance ended. But a friendship continued and with it came regular correspondence eagerly awaited by me and immediately answered on the note paper provided by the International Red Cross. Dorothy's name was well-known to my friends in the camp, and her photograph had a prominent place on the wall beside my bunk.

The Montreal postmark was immediately explained. Dorothy had a brother in the navy who was about to be posted somewhere in Canada for training, and her letter, addressed as usual to an army postbox number in Ottawa, had been posted by him in Montreal, his first port of call.

After the midday meal as I lay on my bunk reading her letter, my attention was distracted by Capaldi's heavy snoring in the next bunk. I looked with distaste at the vibrating lips of my neighbour and the germ of an idea was born. Off came a heavy army boot which I dropped forcefully on Gerry's replete stomach.

'Hey, Gerry. Wake up!' I shouted. Gerry stirred.

'What's the matter?'

'So you think you've got girl friends, eh Gerry? With all that big talk of yours, I don't see any of them coming to Montreal to see you. Catch a load of that postmark.'

I threw the envelope on to Gerry's lap, and showed him the last page of the letter with its signature.

'That's from my girl Dorothy. She's been trying for months to find out where I was, and now she's here to try and get permission to visit me', I paused and added casually. 'She's here with her sister Marion.'

Gerry lay speechless. For two years he hadn't seen a female in the flesh and here was that square Joe Pieri with a girl in Montreal ready to visit him. The great lover was shattered.

'How's she going to manage to see you?', he asked enviously.

'Oh, I'll get to see Duvar tomorrow and try to work out something.'

Next morning I took my place in the office and with the help of some official pretext found myself in O'Connor's room. There I explained my plan to him and gained the consent of the genial Irishman who found the whole thing quite funny. I proceeded to work on Gerry.

'Well Gerry, it's all fixed up for tomorrow in the outside office. Dorothy's coming here and I've been given half an hour's visit.'

'Lucky bugger', snorted Gerry, 'some guys have all the luck.'

That day I made a great play of shaving and grooming myself and strode off jauntily, returning after a suitable interval to give a glowing account of the meeting with my *innamorata*. The seal of truth was put on the story by O'Connor, who, passing by as Gerry was being regaled by a fanciful account of her visit, stopped and remarked, 'That's a really nice girl you have there, 87', and left behind a convinced and goggle-eyed Gerry. I turned the screw a little more.

'You know Gerry, why don't you write a note to Marion? I've told Dorothy all about you, and you might even get the chance of a visit?'

The great lover stirred uneasily, considered the proposal for a brief moment and vanished into the recreation hut, emerging some time later with a sealed envelope in his hand.

'What address will I put?'

He copied with trembling fingers the fictitious address supplied by me. The letter was duly posted, intercepted by O'Connor and read with glee by the half dozen or so people who now knew of the ruse. The gist of the letter was that Gerry was a poor, misinterpreted, prisoner whose soul yearned for contact with the female sex. Although he and Marion had never met, he was sure that they must share some common spiritual bond: would she please answer this poor prisoner and bring a ray of light into his grey sad life behind the barbed wire.

The fulsome letter was answered on pink notepaper obligingly supplied by O'Connor, sprayed with perfume and posted by him in Montreal. Her letter was full of sympathy and solicitude, his answer was immediate and in no time the correspondence developed into a torrid love affair by mail, with Gerry, beside himself with fervour, informing the whole camp of his new Canadian love affair.

His letters increased in passion and desire.

Please Marion I must see you; please try and visit me, please, Marion, please.

But Marion sadly answered that all her pleas had been in vain; no more visits were to be allowed to the camp, and please for her sake, don't approach the colonel.

I'm not supposed to be in Canada at all, and besides I'm leaving for England on the next convoy.

Gerry's despair was great. 'What can I do Joe, what can I do?'

And so we moved to the climax. I returned, downcast, from the office one Saturday morning and sought out Gerry.

'That's Dorothy's last visit, Gerry and the girls leave on Monday for home. Marion would love to see you, even from a distance, so tomorrow around three o'clock they're going to pass over the bridge and give us a wave. I told them you'd be wearing a red scarf on your head and white shorts, so that way they'll know it's you'.

Gerry was grief-stricken. 'Where am I going to get all that gear?'

'No problem', I replied. 'We'll nick a couple of pillowcases from the sick room and Barletta can run you up a pair of shorts in no time. I've brought a bottle of red ink from the office. We'll stain a pillowcase red and you can wear it on your head.'

The next day, Sunday, at about 2.30pm, Gerry and I stood in the middle of the compound, the former bedecked in a pair of white shorts with a red cloth wrapped round his head. The minutes ticked by. Gerry palpitated anxiously. The guards on the machine-gun towers looked curiously at the unusual sight below them, and the camp buzzed with anticipation. At last, high on the bridge above, amongst the strolling passers by on the bridge footpath, I espied two lone female figures who had paused to gaze at the compound below. The odds had paid off, for the chances always were that a couple of females would be out for a walk, and I latched onto the unsuspecting pair to help produce the grand finale.

'There they are, Gerry', I yelled, and through cupped hands bellowed a greeting to the two girls.

'Hello Dorothy. . . hello Marion!' and waved my hands frantically.

The two figures on the bridge paused, leaned over the railings, answering with a wave of hands and handkerchiefs. Gerry went mad.

'It's me Marion, it's me Marion, it's Gerry!'

He cavorted madly, whipped the red cloth from his head, waving it wildly in the air as he shouted the name of his loved one at the top of his voice.

I retreated unobtrusively, leaving the ecstatic Gerry alone in the middle of the arena. Gerry's gyrations increased, his voice rising to a stentorian pitch.

'Oh Marion, it's me...it's me, it's Gerry!' and he whipped the red cloth round his head like a lasso. His wild signals were answered enthusiastically from the bridge until a patrolling guard began to move the girls on, but Gerry's shouts and gyrations diminished not one whit.

Suddenly the gates to the compound opened and in marched the sergeant of the guard flanked by two massive military policemen.

'Grab that guy, we've got another nut here.'

The two MPs took an elbow each, and the startled Gerry was lifted high off the ground then whisked firmly back through the camp gates, leaving us all convulsed with helpless laughter.

Gerry was interrogated at length by the officer of the day on the question of his eccentric behaviour and had his story dismissed as being so improbable as not to warrant further investigation. Moreover, for his impertinence in persisting to take the mickey out of the officer with such a story he was sentenced to five days in the punishment cells.

My deception was never revealed. The non-existent Marion entered the pantheon of Gerry's Goddesses, and for years afterwards during the periodic reunions of old Camp 43 inmates Gerry would recount with great embellishment the story of his unconsummated Canadian love affair!

20
Finale

At the beginning of 1943 the war began to go badly for the Axis countries. The German army had suffered a shattering defeat at Stalingrad and was on the retreat on the Russian front; in North Africa Rommel had been routed at El Alamein and the remnants of the Afrika Korps were soon to surrender in Tunisia. In July the Allied armies landed in Sicily and had entered Palermo with little resistance from what remained of the Italian armed forces.

By the spring of the same year even the most fanatical of the Fascists in the camp had come to the realisation that the war was lost. Nevertheless, in the late summer a small group of die hards amongst them decided on one last gesture of defiance and started on an ambitious plan for a mass escape from the camp. Apart from causing the authorities the maximum possible inconvenience, it was difficult to see what the undertaking could have achieved, for such an exodus would have simply been a pointless escape to nowhere. The plan, however, was a daring one. The recreation hut built by the prisoners in the early days of the camp stood close to the main entrance at a distance of 12 yards or so from the barbed-wire fence. Although the base of the building from the outside seemed to rest flat on the ground, because of the sloping nature of the site there was in fact a space of about two feet between the ground and the floor joists. Work had started here on the digging of a tunnel which was to have its exit some yards beyond the fence on the face of a slope the incline of which would hide any fugitive from the patrolling guards.

Work on the tunnel had been a closely guarded secret known only

FINALE

to the half dozen or so men actively engaged in digging, until one day Pasquale Nardo, my little Sicilian sailor friend, approached and informed me of the proposed escape. A tunnel had been started under a trapdoor cut in the floorboards of a storage cupboard in a corner of the hut. The leaders of the plot were expecting about 20 or so prisoners to take part in the eventual escape. I thanked Pasquale for the information, sat pensively for a moment and did not take long to reach the conclusion that an incident of that nature would be disastrous for myself and for 39 other inmates of the camp.

Some four weeks before, at long last, I had been called to the commandant's office to be informed by Duvar that my parent's efforts back home had finally borne fruit. My release had come through from the Home Office in London, and a group of 40 of us were to be sent back to Britain on the first available convoy. An alternative offer was made to me. At that time the newly formed United Nations Organisation was being set up in San Francisco, and there was a need for personnel who could undertake simultaneous translations in various languages. In those days there were not many who could fit the bill, and although I had no formal education in any language, I had acquired a reputation for quick and accurate interpretation in any combination of English, Italian and German. The colonel was empowered to offer me an initial one-year contract with immediate release.

I was sorely tempted. A whole new world could have been opened up for me. The USA was a melting pot of nationalities where your surname did not matter, or so I believed. What would I find back in Glasgow after a war in which I had been labelled an enemy alien? But my parents back in Glasgow were elderly, and both had struggled to keep the family shop open for their two sons. They had tried long and hard to have me released. There was no question of my going to the UN. I regretfully turned Duvar's offer down and elected to take my place in the group for Britain.

The 40 of us waited impatiently for the date of the departure to be announced. In the meantime we had formed ourselves into a little group of our own for company, for we were regarded with enmity by a small core of die hard Fascists who heaped abuse and taunts of treachery on our heads. We accepted the situation impassively and quite happily, for our great consolation was that we would soon be rid of the hatred and tension of the camp.

But a mass escape from the camp could put our departure in jeopardy, for were it to happen at about the time of the departure, a quarantine would very likely be imposed on the camp until the escaped prisoners had all been recaptured and the matter investigated.

I broke the news to two of my companions also awaiting transportation back to the UK: Joe Guidi, a young restaurateur from Glasgow, and a previous temporary escapee, John Agostini. They agreed that such an escape, if it were to happen before our departure, could well put paid to our hopes of a speedy return home, for God only knew when space could be found for us on another convoy should we be held back for any reason. A direct betrayal of the tunnel to the authorities was absolutely ruled out. The idea of informing on fellow prisoners was dismissed out of hand, no matter what tension there was between us. Also Agostini, with his London gangland background, had no time for narks.

Joe Guidi thought for a while. How would it be if the authorities discovered the tunnel by themselves, in a manner which would implicate and harm no one?

We listened to his idea and agreed. After lights out that night and with all the camp asleep, my two companions and I crept into the recreation hut. We took great pains not to be seen by either prisoners or guards, and in the reflected lights of the perimeter searchlights found and uncovered the trapdoor in the storage cupboard. Leaving Guidi on guard, Agostini and I lowered themselves into the tunnel beneath.

The tunnel had been very skilfully dug out, was about two-foot-high and broad enough to allow a man to wriggle his way forward. A few wooden props sustained the roof, and at the point where it passed under the service road which ran the length of the compound, the props were arranged closely together to compensate for any overhead weight. Working as quickly as possible in the cramped space, Agostini and I stripped away the wooden supports, leaving a 12-foot section under the road completely unsupported. We replaced the trapdoor, retraced our steps and the three of us went back to our bunks to sleep fitfully and to await the morning.

At exactly 6.30am, half an hour before reveille, a large army truck, heavily-laden with provisions, rolled slowly through the

FINALE

gates, and as the wheels crunched over the unsupported tunnel, the earth gave a sigh and collapsed, leaving the truck with its front wheels embedded in the ground. The startled driver leapt from his cab, looked askance at the sunken wheels and was joined by an officer and some other guards. The reaction was swift. The recreation hut was put under armed guard while a swarm of soldiers searched the building until the trapdoor with the entrance to the tunnel was discovered.

Colonel Duvar was no fool. He inspected the entrance to the tunnel personally then listened with interest to the report of the sergeant who had gone a short distance into it. The lorry was pulled out of the hole and the exposed tunnel also inspected. The contented officer summoned the Camp Leader, at that time a Joe Crolla of Edinburgh, to his office. The mystified Camp Leader, who had known nothing of the proposed escape, was informed that in the light of all the circumstances, the discovery of the tunnel and the foiling of the escape plan was satisfaction enough for the authorities, and no further investigation would be necessary. However, as a punishment the recreation hut would be off limits for two weeks, and there the matter would rest.

Furious arguments broke out amongst the conspirators as they sought to apportion blame for the fiasco, uncertain as to whether the tunnel had been tampered with or whether a combination of bad luck and faulty workmanship had caused the ground to subside under the weight of the lorry. But the camp in general had no sympathy for them. The Fascists were now in a small minority, and since the defeat of *Il Duce* was now certain, the fear they had inspired no longer held sway, so they were subjected to the camp's vociferous displeasure for having deprived them of the recreation hut and with it the cinema for two whole weeks.

However, when it came to repairing the section of road where the lorry had come to grief, it became obvious to the dozen or so prisoners who had planned the tunnel that their work had been tampered with. They vowed vengeance on the so-called traitors who had revealed their plan to the enemy. Unknown to us, the absence of my two companions and myself from the dormitory that night had been noted by some of the prisoners and this information got back to the conspirators, who now had clear evidence as to who the saboteurs might be.

ISLE OF THE DISPLACED

Down through the camp grapevine came the threat: those three are going to be dealt with. This was no idle menace. There had been several stabbings in the camp, none of them fatal, but two serious enough to have required the hospitalisation of the victims in a Montreal hospital. Although the assailants had never been identified, it was common knowledge in the camp that they belonged to a hard core of Fascist activists in the merchant seamen group. These were the same ones who had been building the tunnel, and they were threatening vengeance on myself and my two friends.

For the next few days we went in fear of our lives, sleeping in shifts with one always on guard for a possible attack, never separating during the day, wondering whether to seek protection from the authorities. We hoped with every passing hour that the day of our departure from the camp would be announced. It was then that little Pasquale Nardo approached me once again.

Pasquale came from Trapani, a fishing village in Sicily. He was about 30 years old, highly intelligent but almost illiterate. The two of us had been firm friends ever since I had agreed to act as scribe for the little sailor in his correspondence with his aged parents back home who used the local priest as a scribe to write back. It was a measure of the awakening sense of independence of the little sailor that he did not use any of his merchant navy superiors for this service, as did almost all of the illiterate sailors. He preferred to go against all tradition and expectation in such matters and reveal his intimate thoughts to, and place his trust in, an outsider, an *Inglese* such as myself. Pasquale was grateful for my services and for the time I had spent in trying to read books with him, as a result of which he was slowly but surely emerging into a new world of literacy and understanding. He came straight to the point.

'I think you are in trouble, Giuseppe. I want to repay you for your goodness to me in these past years. I want you and your two friends to meet with me and Captain Bonorino and some others tonight.'

That evening a small group assembled in the recreation hall: Guidi, Agostini and I, Captain Bonorino, Pasquale and seven seamen — all of them Sicilian — and all of them involved in the digging of the tunnel. Pasquale began to speak, slowly and in Sicilian-accented Italian.

FINALE

'I am a friend of friends in Trapani, and Giuseppe and his two companions are now my friends. The war is lost and we all want to go home in peace to our families. There are bad people here and to them I say this. If any harm comes to Giuseppe and his two friends through anyone in this camp, I am sworn to seek vengeance for them. If I cannot, then my friends in Trapani will. *È ora di farla finita con queste scemate.*' [1]

He stood for a moment, then with an outstretched hand and pointing finger he gestured towards his silent audience of seven seamen, who slowly rose, nodded to Bonorino then quietly and pensively left the room. Pasquale turned and said to me:

'You don't have to worry now. Nobody will dare to touch you or your friends, for they know that they will certainly pay for it one day if they do. If I cannot make them pay, then my friends and family will and the captain here is my witness.'

The three of us looked on in amazement, and I translated for the benefit of Agostini, who had not understood a word. Captain Bonorino, who had been an interested spectator, explained.

'I don't understand the mentality of these *Meridionali* [2] any more than you do, but I think that you have seen the power of the Sicilian Mafia. It's good to have one as a friend, and nobody wants one as an enemy. I don't think anyone will dare to harm you or your friends now, for if anyone does they will pay dearly for it, no matter how long it will take.'

He paused, put a fatherly hand on my shoulder and said, 'Go home to your family in Scotland, Giuseppe, you are fortunate, for God alone only knows what awaits us after the war in Italy.'

Three weeks later, and without further incident, 40 happy men shook the dust of the compound from their feet for the last time. I took emotional leave of the many friends I had made over the last three years, with a special embrace for Pasquale Nardo. Then I watched the gates of the camp close behind me for the last time as I started on the first leg of the journey back to eventual freedom. A few months after this, Camp 43 ceased to exist as an internment camp. In late July 1943 Mussolini was forced to resign as head of the Italian state, and the new head of government, Marshal Badoglio,

---

[1] 'It's time to call a halt to this nonsense.'
[2] Southerners

immediately surrendered all his armed forces and sued for peace with the Allies. Italians were no longer enemies. The prisoners in what remained of the camp were no longer treated as such. All were offered work of some sort pending the final outcome of the war in Europe and eventual repatriation. Almost en masse the seamen accepted forestry work in the Canadian wilderness, and were dispersed to lumber camps in Quebec and Ontario, as were some of the remaining civilians. Commensurate with their abilities and professions the rest were offered work in the Montreal district where they remained until they could be sent back to their respective homes.

Champlain's old fort on Ile Sainte Hélène now stood empty, and the unmanned and disarmed machine-gun towers gazed down on a deserted and windswept compound.

21
Return

As the bus carrying all 40 of us moved slowly on to the bridge and towards Montreal, heads were craned to catch a last glance of the building and compound that had been our home for the last three years. All of us were strangely silent as Ile Sainte Hélène was left behind, and we did not experience the euphoria that one might have expected in prisoners heading towards their liberty. There was in a way as much uncertainty in the freedom that awaited us as there had been in the confinement we had just left. In Camp 43 situations and neighbours were well-defined and understood, but here we were about to be set free in a society which for three years had labelled us as enemies, kept us strictly quarantined behind barbed wire and had treated us as somehow dangerous.

Moreover, the freedom offered us was conditional, given only on the understanding that each of us would take up some form of work on our return home. Where would we be offered work? Who would be our companions? As released enemies how would we be treated by the civilians with whom we would have to mix? These thoughts troubled me to no small extent and were obviously uppermost too in my comrades' thoughts as the bus drove through the busy city streets towards the station. Where one would have expected animated conversation there was only the odd word between us to break the almost gloomy silence as the bus retraced the route we had taken three years ago. But with what a difference! On our departure from the camp we had been issued with dark blue serge suits, white shirts and dark ties, and we must have looked like well-scrubbed inmates of some institution or other. The contrast with our appearance three years before — unwashed, unshaven and almost in rags, could not have been greater. Instead of six heavily-armed guards per bus, our escort consisted only of an unarmed French-Canadian sergeant who maintained an amiable monologue as he pointed out places of interest in the city to us, for all the world as if he were the courier on a travel excursion .

We were decanted at the Central Railway Station on Boulevard Dorchester, where we waited for our train to arrive, huddled together like sheep afraid of straying from the comfort and safety of the flock. Unlike the train journey to Montreal three years ago, this time we knew our destination. Halifax in Nova Scotia, where we were to be embarked for the Atlantic crossing back to the UK. The crossing loomed anxiously in our minds. The *Ettrick* was only too well remembered, and the gaiety which we finally showed on the train journey served only to mask the underlying anxiety of the group.

At Halifax our sergeant wished us luck, took leave of us, and passed us over to the care of a young corporal. At the port an awesome and reassuring sight met our eyes. Moored at the pier was the huge bulk of the liner *Queen Elizabeth*. Painted a dull grey, its size dwarfed the warehouses and buildings of the port area. Thousands upon thousands of fully kitted troops lined the quay in front of the ship, and we joined the long queue of uniformed men filing up the gangways into her. The soldiers were American, and their bronzed, smartly uniformed appearance was in stark contrast to our own. In our dark blue outfits we stood out like sore thumbs, giving rise to ribald but good natured conjecture as to our identity. On hearing our accents as we spoke amongst ourselves, one wag offered to bet a dollar that we were Scottish missionaries, scrubbed and disinfected so as not to be contaminated by our proximity to the soldiers, a description which raised gales of laughter.

The journey across the Atlantic was swift and uneventful. The *Queen Elizabeth* was unescorted, her speed more than sufficient protection against U-boat attack. Fitted out as a troopship she could carry 15,000 men and their equipment across the ocean in just over three days and she was a marvel of organisation on board. The men slept in cabins from which all furniture had been removed, each of which could accommodate 40 men in hammocks. To facilitate movement, all the doors had been taken away as well and during emergency drill the sleeping quarters could be evacuated in a matter of minutes.

RETURN

The feeding of such a mass of people was a masterpiece of logistics. Each area was allocated a number, and the day would start with a call over the Tannoy system. 'Zone 1, first call for chow' and the first group would form a queue to move towards the galley area, there to be issued with a metal tray of food to be eaten when seated in any available space on deck. Then a queue formed for washing-up places to clean the utensils. Five hours later, we repeated the process once more.

Latrine requirements had been solved by the erection of a row of wooden toilet seats over the side of the ship round the complete circumference of the lower deck, providing hundreds of sea-going equivalents of dry lavatories. It was while seated on one of these on the afternoon of July 27 that I heard over the Tannoy of the downfall of Mussolini and of Italy's surrender to the Allies. I wondered what the reaction would be back in Camp 43 amongst the Fascist remnant there, and wondered too of what use Malusa's little black book would be to him now.

The next day the *Queen Elizabeth* docked at Greenock. Our group disembarked, and still under the supervision of our corporal, mounted a train which took us south to Liverpool, there to stand on the same quay from which we had climbed on to the *Ett*rick three long years ago. There we boarded a large ferry for the short crossing to the Isle of Man. My release had been conditional on taking up some form of work of national importance. Under this category came farming and any other form of food production, and having opted for work of this type, I had the choice of having a work place found for me by my parents near home. Failing this, one would be allocated to me by the authorities in any part of the UK. One month's grace was allowed for work to be found, the waiting period to be spent as an internee on the Isle Of Man.

Most of the returning Camp 43 prisoners had been given similar conditions for their release, so I was still with my colleagues as they boarded the ship that was to take them to the island. On this journey, however, there were no guards, no barbed wire and no claustrophobic confinement in a hold. For the short journey we had the freedom of the ship and could mix freely with the passengers, most of whom were Italians and Germans of both sexes and of all ages on their way to visit relatives in the various camps on the island.

ISLE OF THE DISPLACED

The contrast between Camp 43 and the camps on the Isle of Man could not have been greater. On the Isle of Man internment zones had been formed by wiring off areas of terraced houses and small hotels and designating them as camps. Two or three men shared each bedroom, and toilet facilities and living accommodation were more than adequate. There was space in abundance. We were assigned to the Onchan Camp, and to 'the Canadians', as we were immediately christened by the men there, the place had the appearance of a holiday camp!

A man could live as a human being in Onchan Camp. You wore your own civilian clothes, not a prisoner's uniform. You slept in a civilised bedroom and ate in a proper dining room. You did not have to share a cramped and stuffy dungeon-like dormitory with a hundred flatulent, coughing, swearing and often unwashed companions, and you did not have to share a latrine with 20 other men.

You had sitting rooms to lounge in, with newspapers and books to read and a radio to listen to. You had no machine-gun towers menacing your every move and no sergeant Le Seour to make your life a misery. You could find privacy if desired and did not have to rub shoulders constantly with persons you disliked and yet could not avoid. You could go to work on one of the many farms on the island and be left alone there all day, and not be herded into closely guarded work parties to serve as objects of curiosity for the local inhabitants. And most important of all, you could have visitors and see and talk with your loved ones.

The only inferior aspect of life on the Isle of Man was the food. Compared to the cornucopia of all good things in Camp 43, rations there were plain and not overabundant, but in this the internees fared no worse than the general population of Britain in wartime. There was no doubt in my mind that I would have preferred a three-year diet of bread and cheese and water on the Isle of Man than a three-year stay in Camp 43 with its superabundance of good food. But I was to learn later that Italians of my age and of similar circumstances were released after only a few month's internment there, to take up some form of work as free men. If only I had lied with my feet three years before at Woodhouselea!

At the beginning the short stay in Onchan Camp was sheer luxury for me. I shared a room with two other 'Canadians', and we never ceased to marvel at the difference of life in the two camps. There was

RETURN

no strict routine imposed on us. Roll-call consisted of a visit and a cursory inspection of the room by a sergeant, after which you were as free as a bird to do as you pleased within the confines of the camp. If you felt like some work in the fresh air you presented yourself at the gate in the morning after breakfast, to be picked up by a lorry and left for a day's work at one of the hundreds of farms which dotted the island. This work would be supervised only by the local farmer and we were treated at all times in a friendly and pleasant manner. The day's work over, the lorry did its rounds of the farms and returned the day workers to the camp. No fuss, no armed guards, no shouted orders, no push and shove. The contrast could not have been greater.

My first act once settled in Onchan Camp was to send off a letter to my family, and my father immediately applied for permission to visit. Although travel in wartime Britain was not easy, within four days of the receipt of my news, father and son met in the visitor's room at Onchan. The meeting was probably the most emotional moment of my internment. A man in his sixties can age considerably in the space of three years, and I was shocked at the change in my father's appearance. The still virile, thickset man I remembered was suddenly frail and trembling, with a thin voice and shrunken neckline, and I was saddened at the realisation that the war and the uncertainty of his son's fate had taken their toll.

22
Aftermath

One week later, with travel permit in pocket, I was a completely free man, standing alone in a Liverpool railway station waiting for the Glasgow train. For the first time in three years I was not under some form of military constraint or other. I had been left completely to my own resources and free to move about as I pleased. The sensation was a strange and frightening one. I could feel anxiety and apprehension well up inside me, and for a brief moment I almost wished I were back in the compound of Camp 43 surrounded by all the well-known and now strangely comfortable elements of that environment.

Sudden release from captivity can be almost as traumatic as the shock of arrest. The suddenness of my imprisonment had cut me off without warning from my family and friends and the environment I had always known. As a prisoner, the routine duties of having to earn a living and making a way for myself in life had stopped. Life was organised forcibly for me and I no longer needed to take responsibility for myself. Existence was merely a long round of killing time and waiting for an uncertain future, with my destiny no longer in my own hands. I simply had to obey orders and do exactly as I was told; I had become effectively depersonalised.

With my release, the tensely wound psychological spring which had enabled me to come to terms with my captivity and completely subservient way of life seemed to have suddenly unwound. I was free and depending purely on my own resources. There was no one there to tell me what to do or how to do it, no one to pull me by the arm or give me a nudge with a rifle butt, no armed soldier to order me brusquely on to a train.

With a tight knot in my stomach I looked around at the others waiting with me on the platform. These were people who for the last three years had looked upon me as a dangerous enemy. What would their reaction be if they knew who and what I was? I longed for the sight of a familiar face, of a familiar figure to turn and talk to. There were a few civilians standing about, but in the main the waiting passengers were military personnel of both sexes, weighed down by their kit, either going or returning from leave. They stood in groups chatting and laughing, and I felt the complete outsider, afraid to engage in conversation in case my status be discovered and my identity as an enemy alien made known to all.

In the packed train compartment I politely refused the many offers of cigarettes and sandwiches from fellow travellers. I fended off their attempts at conversation as non-committally and as politely as I could, and then, so as not to have to participate in their exchange of introductions and small talk, pretended to fall asleep. The pretence turned to reality and I did sleep, to be jolted awake by the jerking of the train as it drew into Glasgow's Central station. It was dark on the platform as I stepped down from the compartment. I had forgotten about the blackout, and in the dim light I did not at first recognise the uniformed figure approaching alongside the train. Slightly more grizzled and greyer than three years before and now in a police inspector's uniform was my father's old friend Alex McCrae. His hand reached out and shook mine.

'So you're back now, Joe. How's it going?'

I was immediately put at ease by his friendly greeting, and as he escorted me out of the station I was amazed to see parked at the edge of the pavement a dark box-like Black Maria, of the type used in my arrest. Alex laughed at my look of startled surprise.

'We'll bring you back the same way we brought you in!'

But this time I sat in the front of the van beside Alex and the driver, and the journey home was much longer. My parents had gone to live in Bearsden, on the outskirts of Glasgow, and in the blackout I don't know how I could have managed to find my way there without the help of Black Alex. The van crawled its way along the blacked-out streets, following the barely visible tram tracks for direction, and the slow journey gave me just a little idea of what life must have been like in the winter in wartime Glasgow. Alex kept on chatting, giving me news of old friends. Do you remember so-and-so? Well, he was shot down and killed over France. And so-and-so?

He died on a torpedoed merchant ship. And so-and so? Well, he's still around somewhere, as far as I know. And Sergeant Santangeli? He was badly wounded at El Alamein. And the realisation dawned on me that despite everything, I had been one of the lucky ones.

Slowly and tentatively I edged my way back into society. My parents were overjoyed to see me alive and well, with mother crying tears of happiness every day and saying rosary after rosary of thanks for the return of her son. Despite their advancing years they had managed to keep the shop going, opening two days a week without help, paying the rent so that their sons could have something to come back to after war's end. They had nothing but praise for their neighbours, for despite their obvious Italian origin no harsh words had ever been addressed to them. For my part I was glad that my father had taken out British nationality when he did. Given the indiscriminate nature of the early arrests, he too might well have finished up behind barbed wire. Not in the best of health, he might not have survived the trauma of the first weeks of internment and the dreadful conditions at Warth Mills, where, as I was to learn later, several old men had died.

I had been allocated a job on a farm in Summerston, near Glasgow, and enjoyed the hard but healthy work there. The owner, Tom McClymont, a dour honest Scot, treated me no differently from the rest of his workers, the bulk of whom were Land Army girls who didn't seem to care one jot what my background was, and the months spent in that environment went a long way to easing the feeling of estrangement within me. Ironically, even on that farm there were times when I could almost feel myself back in Camp 43. Near to Glasgow, at Garelochhead, an Italian PoW camp had been set up, and at times lorry-loads of prisoners were brought to the farm to help in the work. I would then take up my old role as interpreter, much to the delight of Tom McClymont, who was thereby relieved of the frustration of having to mime instructions to his Italian workers. I felt quite close to those PoWs. It hadn't been so long since I had been in the position they were in, and I sympathised fully with them.

In the course of time I began to make contact with old friends and acquaintances, a process which I did not hurry and which I did not initiate. For obvious reasons I preferred them to make the first approach, and all who did seemed genuinely glad to see me. Not one harsh or insulting word did I hear, the one irritant being the constantly repeated enquiry as to how I had enjoyed my stay in Canada, as if I had been on holiday there. But then as I began to realise the sacrifices and suffering everyone had undergone during those years of war, I could see that they might well consider me lucky in my experiences.

The war ended. Although I was still obliged to continue in some form of 'nationally important' work, I began to think of the possibility of taking some tentative steps back into the family business which had been kept barely alive on a very restricted basis by my aged parents. Had I gone by the book and made representations through official channels, the necessary official permits would have been an age in coming (as I had learned from the experience of others). So I parted amicably with Tom McClymont and obtained official permission to go to work as a labourer at a nearby piggery. I then struck a very happy arrangement with the owner. Rather than him pay me £3 per week, I paid him the same sum to present myself for a half hour each morning and then be allowed the rest of the day as a free agent to go about my own affairs. My little deception did not worry me. I felt that I was doing more good all round by helping to feed a hungry populace rather than a bunch of pigs. Although I began to run the shop from the wings, as it were, I hesitated quite some time before taking up work openly. Even when eventually given official permission to go back to the family business I did not have the courage to face people across a counter, feeling that internment had left a visible stigma attached to me.

Remarkably enough, when I did go back to serving the public, I found that attitudes seemed to have been transformed. Complete strangers, ex-soldiers who had fought in the Italian campaigns and who correctly assumed that I was Italian, would regale me with their stories of Italy. Of how they were treated as liberators, of the hospitality received from Italian families, of the help given to escaped British prisoners and of the friendliness of the population in general. For whatever reason, the war seemed to have broadened attitudes and increased people's tolerance. Paradoxically, after all that had happened, for the first time in my life I began to feel welcome and a part of the society in which I lived.

At the end of 1945 my brother Ralph was demobbed, and together we applied ourselves to the family shop and the eventual expansion of the business, and in this I never had the impression that the fact of my Italian background mattered in any way.

In 1950, after a three-year courtship I married a local girl, Mary Cameron, who, after the initial hand-wringing histrionics of my mother, became a much loved member of our family. Our marriage gave us four children, all of whom became university graduates in medicine, law and in the arts. I often wondered if their Italian name and background had ever been a disadvantage to them in any way, or if they had ever been subjected to slights and insults because of it. My question on the subject had no meaning for them and drew blank stares. There was, after all, a world of difference in growing up in the Gorbals in the 1920s and growing up in Bearsden in the 1960s.

But although I was happy and pleased that they had never been subjected to any of the slights and insults common to me in my youth, I was, I must admit, somewhat surprised. Xenophobia is not the prerogative of any one social group or of any one nation. Indeed, although covert, it is probably much more prevalent in the various establishments that strive to maintain the social status quo. In this country one has only to look at the nomenclature used to describe resident foreigners. 'Foreigner' does not suffice. One has to be an 'alien', a word of somewhat sinister, extraterrestrial connotations. But perhaps I reveal a shade of paranoia in saying this.

23
Endings

Ile Sainte Hélène has changed considerably since 1940. In 1967 the island was used as the site for the Montreal World Exhibition; its area was almost doubled by earth and rock infills for the purpose of building pavilions for Expo 67 and it is now accessible by a modern metro system. *La Poudrière*, the Powderhouse, which had served as the workshop for the manufacture of packing crates, is now a permanent theatre, much used for municipal and national productions. Champlain's old fort still stands. It now serves as a war museum and is a popular tourist attraction. The hard earth which had served the prisoners as a compound has become a well-tended lawn. At the front, in place of the forbidding barbed-wire fence there is now a row of tall trees which unfortunately block out the view of the city across the river. The massive Jacques Cartier bridge still looms unchanged over the site. The dormitories, in reality no more than long narrow passages, are now hung with military exhibits, while the kitchen and refectory areas also serve the same purpose.

Although cleaned and well-varnished, the original punishment cells remain, with the brass plaque and its reference to dangerous Nazi and Fascist prisoners well in evidence. On seeing the plaque for the first time I could not restrain an unbelieving chuckle as I remembered the ones who had spent time in those cells: the 'fool' Ciritiello, Barleta the tailor, Barsi the runner, Gerry the lover, Martinez, Festa and myself. Only one Fascist, and a not very dangerous one at that, among the lot! The first casualty in war is indeed truth!

For many years after the war I kept in touch with many of the friends made on Ile Sainte Hélène. Pasquale Nardo, the little Sicilian returned to his native Trapani for a while. He then went north to

Naples, where he built up a thriving fruit exporting business, and now, elderly, affluent and very literate, I last saw him driving off happily in his Alfa Romeo. I could not help wondering if his Mafia connections had been of help to him, but there was something in his newly-acquired sophistication which made me hesitate to ask.

Captain Bonorino was pensioned off at the war's end and retired to his little villa high on the hills overlooking Genoa where I visited him occasionally with my family until his death in the 1960's. His hobby was wine-making, and many an exquisite glass we drank whilst exchanging tales of Camp 43. It is a curious aspect of human psychology that very often the mind tends to ignore the negative aspects of past experiences and in reminiscing dwells only on the more pleasant ones. The stories swapped in any gathering of the old prisoners seemed to deal only with the humorous aspects of life there. The antics of the sailor Baldino in front of the cinema screen, the exploits of Gerry Capaldi, the preening and vanity of Moramarco, the nostalgic songs sung in the compound in the warm summer evenings, Bosco the mascot and his roll-call gift to Captain Pitblado. And yet seldom a mention of the awful Warth Mills, the fear and danger on the *Ettrick*, the brutality of the first night on the island, and the crushing, soul-destroying uncertainty and boredom of life in the camp.

After the closure of the camp, George Martinez worked for a time as a draughtsman in a Montreal office. The war ended, he returned to his home in Romsey, where he lives to this day. There he set up a company for the manufacture of wire-making machinery and achieved a considerable success in the world of industry. He was reunited with his fiancée Mariolina, married, raised a family and now enjoys the company of his many grandchildren.

The priests were all released in Canada. Father Roffinella went to St Michael's college in Toronto, Father Frizzero resumed his duties as a Xavierian missionary, while Father Schlisizzi gave up the priesthood, married and started a career as University lecturer. Barleta of the bicycle escapade returned to Scotland, opened up a little restaurant in Glasgow where he now lives in retirement. An old man, in the summer he sits on a park bench, reliving camp memories in the occasional chats we have together. Romeo Capitanio, whose presence in the camp was so unobtrusive and yet so invaluable, returned to London and to his position at the Credit Lyonnaise in Lombard

ENDINGS

Street and to the care of his mother. The entrance to his bank bore a constant reminder of his dead father, for the two statues of Hercules which support the massive portals of the building were sculpted and placed there by him. It seems as if destiny lays a tragic hand on some families, for in the late 1960s, overtaken by who knows what personal demon, Romeo too died by his own hand.

O'Connor Lynch went to live in Greenwich village in New York City. One day in the early 1960s he was mugged and robbed of his wallet, sustaining severe injuries in the incident. He recovered, bought a beautiful house in Scarsdale, but his health was never the same. His art collection, amassed so cheaply in Italy before the war, is now worth millions and is permanently housed in the Art Gallery of the State University of New York. He developed Parkinson's disease, and finally died in 1977. My wife and I paid several visits to his home, the last one only a few months before his death.

During one of these visits I was told a remarkable story. In his capacity as camp interpreter and censor of mail, O'Connor had access to the civilian prisoners' dossiers, which seemingly had arrived in Canada from the UK about a year after our arrests. In my dossier the following fact was recorded. In 1935 an aunt of mine living in St Paul, Minnesota had made me a present of a five-year subscription to *Time* magazine, the now famous news magazine. In those years *Time* did not have an international circulation, and was not available on the news-stands here, so I received my subscription copies through the post. Round about 1935, these copies began to arrive with pages missing from the foreign news section. I wrote to the magazine, at that time published in Chicago, complaining about this, and a few weeks later, in a plain envelope, I received the missing pages. They dealt with the affair between King Edward and Mrs Simpson, news of which had been studiously kept from the British public. *Time* magazine was considered by the government of the time as having Fascist sympathies, and any copies arriving here were subjected to rigorous censorship. The fact that I was a subscriber to the magazine was recorded in my dossier. So not only was I an Italian, but I was also a reader of *Time* magazine. If only my aunt could have known how much she had contributed to my war-time predicament!

Sam Corti was demobbed in 1946 and returned to his café in Glasgow. On one of the walls of his shop there hangs a photograph of himself as a sergeant in the British Army. Prominently displayed in the privacy of his own home there is a framed photograph of his day of glory in Rome.

Festa and Malusa were never heard of again, and since the latter's little black book could not be put to use, I presume it was burned. After the war it was virtually impossible to find anyone who would admit to having been a Fascist in Italy, so Malusa's political fanaticism could possibly have espoused the Christian Democratic cause.

Aldo Girasole, who shared my cell on the night of my arrest, and who objected to the Alsatian's ministrations at the time of our welcome at the camp, returned home with the first batch of prisoners to leave at the time of Paterson's visit, and was finally re-united and married to his fiancée. He was able to restart his business and prospered, only to die when comparatively young in his sixties. His son Aldo carries on the family business, and is prominent in the activities of the Scottish-Italian Golfing Society.

Ralph Taglione, ex-manager of the Café Royale, was released in Canada where he set up a flourishing importation business which does a lot of business in fruit with Naples. John Agostini returned to London, where he set up a profitable bookies' business. Barocas, the astronomer, returned to his position at Greenwich observatory, and could be seen occasionally on TV in the late fifties and early sixties describing the functions of the newly-developed artificial satellites.

As for me, to this day I still travel with a Italian passport. The conditioning of childhood dies hard, the dichotomy instilled in me from my long-past Gorbals' years persists, and although I often wish I had a flag to wave patriotically, I have to be content with a chameleon-like personality which allows me to blend into either background, Scottish or Italian. The skirl of bagpipes, the sight of a mist-shrouded Highland landscape, the roar of Scottish football fans singing *O Flower of Scotland*, the simple beauty of a Burns' poem set to music — all these things can stir my soul. And yet the same emotions can be aroused in me by the view from some Tuscan hilltop town, the scent of olive groves and vineyards, and by the music which is part and parcel of life in a small Italian town.

For I am probably neither one thing nor the other. Perfectly at home amongst my Scottish friends and relations as I am, I can still be jolted apart by a perfectly innocent question which places me squarely into an Italian context.

'Are you going home for your holidays this year, Joe?'

And if I am on holiday in Italy my friends and relations there greet me with the friendly cry, *'É arrivato il vecchio Scozzese'*.[1]

The world has changed out of all recognition during the years since the end of the war, and Barga and its surroundings have changed with it. The grinding poverty which once forced its sons to seek a life in other lands no longer exists, and the poor crofts which once dotted the neighbouring hills have long since vanished. Barga is now wealthy and prosperous. The area has become a Mecca for tourists seeking the flavour of Tuscany, and posters of the town in all its breathtaking beauty can be seen in travel agencies throughout Europe.

Mary and I visit from time to time. We sit in a little bar in the piazza, where we can observe the passing tourists and reminisce with one or other of our few remaining contemporaries. From our table I can look up to the hills of Bacchionero, my birthplace. But I no longer take the long trek up there to enjoy the tranquillity and admire the view down into the valley. The path has become too steep.

---

[1] 'The old Scotsman has arrived.'

Epilogue

The war of nearly 60 years ago was probably the most important event in the lifetime of my generation. Our world then was torn apart, shattered and altered in the most dramatic manner imaginable by forces over which we had no control. Millions of young men died in battle and millions more died as civilians in bombed cities and in Nazi extermination camps and it is against horrors like these that one's own personal experiences in the war have to be judged. By these criteria I had a very easy and very lucky war. Only for a very short time was I in great physical danger, and one can become resigned to and accept a long period of confinement, no matter how uncomfortable or unjustified that confinement may be.

My internment had its positive aspects. It gave me a whole new set of values by which I was finally able to live at ease with my status as a foreign immigrant. I came to realise that it is not flags or nations that are important, but people and the human relationships they form. I won't ever forget the old ticket collector at the station in Garrioch Road with his gift of cigarettes and his remarks about Jock Tamson's bairns. Or Dino Orsi and his sharing of chocolate bars at Woodhouselea. Or the soldier on the *Ettrick*, whose name I shall never know, who kept his promise by telling my parents back in Glasgow that I was alive and well. Or Pasquale Nardo, the little Sicilian sailor who protected me from the *Fascisti*. Or Black Alex McCrae waiting at Central Station for me with a Black Maria.

In 1940 he had warned me that they were coming to take me away and he was there in 1943 to take me home.